A Career Podiatric Medicine

A step in the right direction

David R Tollafield

Tollafield

First published 2023
Published by Busypencilcase Communications
Est. 2015

Copyright © 2023 David R Tollafield

All rights reserved. No part of this publication may be reproduced, stored in a retrieval system, or transmitted in any form or by any means without the written permission of the author, nor otherwise circulated in any form of binding or cover other than that which it is published and without a similar condition being imposed on the subsequent publisher.

ISBN: 9798843600259

Cover design created by Petya Tsankova

Features author talking to students and working in an operating theatre. Private podiatry practice suite. Unless stated, all images are licensed under Shutterstock.com

A CAREER IN PODIATRIC MEDICINE
A step in the right direction

This is a career guide aimed at school students aged 13-18, careers teachers graduates and those who might be a little more mature chosing to enter podiatry through the newer routes toward a degree.

Written in six sections this guide is designed to be 'general' and may vary from institution to institution as well as use different terminology for the course curriculum.

Sections 1 and **2** may appeal to younger students from 13 years, while older students, having completed GCSE sciences or access courses, will find **Section 3** covers university education with tips. **Section 4** looks at the scope of podiatry while **Section 5** takes the reader into the postgraduate areas and sub-specialisms. **Section 6** provides additional information at the back of this book to cover contacts, NHS pay scales together with a comprehensive glossary of terms after Section 6.

The author does not recommend one university over another and all universities mentioned were invited to comment on the content of this book. However, you are advised to check each university for guidance on their entry requirements, view their prospectus and website for further information.

Material contained in this book was correct at the time of publication.

Views held are those of the author(s) and do not necessarily represent those of the Royal College of Podiatry (RCoP), Institute of Chiropodists & Podiatrists (IOCP) or the Health & Care Professions Council (HCPC). Every effort has been made to include the views of all UK podiatry courses within this book.

D R Tollafield,
Editor-Author-Podiatrist

FIREFLY
CUSTOM MADE FOOT ORTHOSES
PODIATRIC MSK BIOMECHANICS
www.fireflyorthoses.com

CONTENTS

Introduction - A Health Profession to Serve with Pride 9
Pathfinder 10

1 - MAKING THAT CAREER CHOICE 13

A Healthy Career – discover podiatry 15
How did they get into podiatry? 17
Stepping into a new career 20

2- PODIATRY IS A MEDICAL SUBJECT 23

Podiatry looks beyond the foot 25
Working in clinical practice 27
Advancing your clinical career 31
Opportunities outside the NHS 35
Job availability in podiatry 38
The NHS Podiatrist 39

3- STUDYING PODIATRY AT UNIVERSITY: *THE NUTS & BOLTS* ... 41

Selecting a university in the United Kingdom 42
Transforming from school to university 45
Reflective thoughts from podiatry students 46
Reading Podiatric Medicine 49
The Importance of Science in Podiatry on Entry 51
Defining Clinical Skills 53
Placements versus On-Site Clinics 57
The Bachelor Degree Curriculum 61
What people say about the Course 63
Anatomical dissection 69
Examination and Assessment 72
The Dissertation & Thesis 73
Learning to Speak in Public 77
Which direction to go after qualifying? 78
After graduation 79
Advanced techniques 80
Children's Podiatry 83
Dermatology 85
Independent prescribing (I.P.) 87

Overseas and work experience	91
Podiatry on the Move	97
Gender and diversity	99
Course Education Costs	101
The Apprenticeship Scheme	104
Books & Journals	106

4 - PODIATRISTS SERVING THE NATION'S FOOT HEALTH 109

Where do you start?	110
What we do and what we would like to do	113
Making a Career Plan	115
What does a General Practitioner in Podiatry Do?	117
The Softer Side of Podiatry	118
A Common Feature in Feet	119
The Clinic and Caseload	121
The Home Visit	125
The National Health Service	128
Moving Up the Ladder in the NHS	131
Extended Scope Practitioners	132
The Vascular Practitioner	141
Cancer management	144
Rheumatology	146
High-Risk Podiatry	152
What makes a specialist in high-risk	154
Musculoskeletal Podiatry	156
Prison Work	158
Footwear and research	160
Pic 'n Mix	162
Independent Practice v Employment	164
New models of advancement in health care	165

5- THE DEVELOPING PROFESSION OF PODIATRY 169

	170
The Business End of Podiatry	170
Developing a Modern Practice	171
Gait Analysis	174
Management in the NHS	175
Podiatric Sports Medicine	177

DANCE AND PODIATRY	180
PODIATRIC SURGERY	183
EXPERT WITNESS AND PODIATRY	189
FORENSIC PODIATRY	192
THE EDUCATIONALIST	194
RESEARCH AS A CAREER	198

6 - CLOSING NOTES AND HELPFUL STUFF 201

QUICK HISTORY OF PODIATRY	211
ACKOWLEDGEMENTS	213
ABOUT THE AUTHOR	216
UNLESS MENTIONED, ALL BOOKS ARE AVAILABLE THROUGH AMAZON BOOKS	221
INDEX	222

A full glossary of terms used can be found at the end of this book – pages 204 - 210 to save googling or looking up technical words.

University of
Southampton
MAKE A DIFFERENCE
TO HEALTHCARE
STUDY BSc PODIATRY AT THE UNIVERSITY OF SOUTHAMPTON AND BECOME A CAREER-READY PODIATRIST EQUIPPED TO JOIN AND LEAD A GLOBAL COMMUNITY.
+ Join the highest ranked university in the world offering BSc Podiatry*
+ Gain 1,000 hours of clinical experience across diverse practice placements
+ Develop your skills in our superb multi-functional skills suites
+ Learn the science to treat and manage lower limb disorders
+ Take part in world-leading programmes of research
*QS World University Rankings, 2023
ACCREDITED BY THE ROYAL COLLEGE OF PODIATRY AND APPROVED BY THE HEALTH AND CARE PROFESSIONS COUNCIL (HCPC)
FIND OUT MORE
@HSciences

Introduction - A Health Profession to Serve with Pride

Podiatry is a career that takes you places.

Many have found podiatry by accident. This medical foot health career is rarely found on the career library shelf. Podiatrist Alexander Lawson-Duff blogged recently, *'Podiatry really is a career that can take you places'* - while another podiatrist, Jolie Beattie, correctly suggests - *'Podiatry is the footpath to many careers.'*

> You can come out and have an earning capacity immediately and the status of the science graduate with the honours as well. **Louise Kennedy.**

If you are interested in health as a career, you may be surprised that podiatry is more than feet alone. If you want to explore a career in health care, don't just look at medicine, dentistry, nursing or physiotherapy.

COMPARE ALL ASPECTS OF PODIATRIC MEDICINE BEFORE COMMITTING TO A FINAL DECISION

The Importance of Quality Information

Sadly, some fifty per cent of the material available on the internet misrepresents podiatry. Of the material that could be helpful, such descriptions are superficial and seem to portray podiatry as an afterthought and, in some cases, more akin to 'pedicure.'

Podiatry does have repetitive elements, but even the most exciting of occupations repeat common activities. However, podiatry can bring a different face and daily challenge, testing our resolve as clinicians.

With the help of seventy people; students, lecturers, clinicians and researchers in podiatry, we will take you on a journey. My colleagues and friends set out to create a reference about a profession we have all come to love, told by colleagues who have shaped their destiny in podiatry. This is the first of a two-part series. The companion book *'Voices from Podiatric Medicine – Career journeys past and present,'* carries the full story from many who have contributed to this book.

Pathfinder

Reflecting on her personal choice
> There was the diabetes side, which is a big category and the vascular side. There was paediatrics and sports medicine. After the musculoskeletal stuff, there was surgery, then dermatology. Things have advanced, and we can do more in the way of imaging with ultrasound or we examine gait analysis training, deal with cosmetic podiatry - making the feet look better. You can take part in events like the London Marathon, Commonwealth Games, the Olympic Games. So there are lots of different kinds of interesting career pathways. I started off in the NHS as most of us do. I was there for a good nine, ten years, and that was invaluable. There were some fantastic parts within that, in that my interest was the musculoskeletal side of things, the biomechanics, the gait analysis, and the sports injuries associated with that, but also paediatrics and the developmental side of it as well. So there are lots of different arms to that fork that I could go down. The good thing for me was that at that point we could pretty much mould a career we wanted, but with insight into some areas that weren't necessarily my interest area but were important, such as the vascular clinics, the dermatology clinics, the rheumatoid clinics, the diabetes clinics, and all of which would inform everyday practice. **Claire Carr** (Independent Podiatrist)

Jewel in the crown
> From job security to an exciting range of specialisms, podiatry is the hidden jewel that can unlock a fulfilling career. From private practice to NHS, dermatology, sports, diabetes to surgery, the range and scope is vast and there is never a boring day. It may not seem as glamorous, and the old rumour that all podiatrists do is simple routine care could not be further from the truth; it's an evolving and dynamic profession. As I always say to my patients – everyone has feet and they all go wrong at some point – it reinforces the exciting times and future of the profession. **Usamah Khalid** (Trainee Podiatrist in surgery)

Employment Categories – quick reference

Independent – Private sector, clinics, hospital, nursing homes, Business and Development Manager
National Health Service – General podiatry, extended scope high risk, podiatric surgery, managerial
Industrial – Outside the usual mediums of practice often local, short-term

contract or employed by non-formal bodies e.g Shuropody

Education & Research– Lecturer and researcher, clinical demonstrator, Head of Department or School

Figure 1 (below) provides an overview of the opportunities available to podiatrists. The darker circles represent general activities based around health screening. The surrounding circles offer career opportunities while the hexagonal boxes are the focal areas for employment. Modern podiatry allows a blend of working across different areas. All students should understand that a wide choice is available to graduates after qualifying.

Figure 1

Career Opportunities

Modern University buildings provide quality libraries and resources

Universities of Southampton and Huddersfield

In Pursuit of a Career in Podiatric Healthcare?

1 - Making that Career Choice

With so many options at 13, it's tough to make that decision before leaving school at 18.

I know – I was there once, and my path was not podiatry; at the time podiatry did not exist as it does today. Your career adviser may not even come up with podiatry as a career choice because there is so little quality information available to make a strong suggestion, let alone compare with other career options. However, if you are keen on 'health care,' this book is for you. Even if you don't think podiatry attracts your interest, check out the information and be prepared to be surprised.

So why not make Podiatry your career choice?

> Do something that you love and then everything else will take care of itself. You won't be clock watching. You will be just enjoying your work, and people come and pay you good money anyway to do that stuff that you love. I can say that I have never had a day at work that I didn't want to be there. **Jennifer Muir** *(Independent Podiatrist)*

Next check out some useful criteria next to help you consider your career.

Do you fit these criteria?

Need, challenge, opportunity, and financial reward & security.

<u>Key elements of need</u>

- Are you looking for a health-based career – treating patients?
- Do you need a stable career programme?
- Do you desire to use your sciences?
- Is there an academic opportunity after graduation?
- Can you seek personal guidance (mentorship) within your career choice?
- Is there a career progression ladder you need?

<u>Challenging yourself</u>

- Is there room for new developmental ideas in this career?
- Are you an innovator and can you be independent?
- Do you mind working with risk?
- Do you want to work with a team or on your own?
- Do the curriculum and qualifications allow you to progress?

<u>Opportunity beyond the career</u>

- Would you want to travel with your career?
- Can you work in industry?
- Does your career provide leadership opportunities?

<u>Financial reward & security</u>

- Can you find a job in a stable labour market?
- Do you feel that you will provide a level of financial security?
- Does your career provide you with independence – autonomy for decision-making?

Podiatry provides for all the above. Let's look into podiatry with a little more detail.

A Healthy Career – discover podiatry

There are some assumptions

- First, you are interested in a health career with an emphasis on science and biology
- The second assumption is that you want a career. One that is more than a 'job', one that is enjoyable, one that provides an income, one that is flexible and one that ideally provides you with a good lifestyle and stability
- Maybe you want an opportunity to teach, undertake research or study for a doctorate. Lead a team, run a practice as a business, develop management skills, work with a football team, a dance centre or even the law
- Perhaps you would like the opportunity to travel, to speak nationally or internationally, or become a well-known author

These choices are open to you in podiatry.

A job for life?

No one expects a job for life these days, but the skills you accrue with training will persuade you that this profession is one you can sink into a life's investment. Many careers offer some, if not all, of the benefits described. Podiatry overlaps with skills seen in medicine and dentistry.

What makes podiatry unique is the opportunity to keep your own independence and yet work with a team of other health care professionals. You can work part-time, or full-time, work for the NHS or the independent sector (private practice) or work for companies. There is a section called Mix 'n Match later on, advising how to use a blend of employment opportunities.

The current qualification of a Bachelor of Science degree can open other doors. For example, advanced training (with a Master's Degree) will allow you to become a consultant podiatric surgeon, or lead you into research or teaching to gain a doctorate and maybe even a professorship. Podiatry (podiatric medicine) can offer all of this, motivating its members to reach their potential. The most important fact for the school leaver is that you can do well and be your own boss.

Nothing comes to us without effort. It is unlikely that any health profession will make you instantly rich. Being rich may appear ideal but in reality, being rich also comes from enjoying what you do - quality of life does not require money, although it helps. A desire to get out of bed each day with an aspiration to go to work is important. A job that is no longer a job but a hobby – a passion, means you know you have reached your goal. That is what podiatry has been to me.

> I qualified in 1978 and found myself drawn into many new fields. But there are other exciting roles if surgery is not your thing. Fifty years has seen a massive change. Today it is a profession with a robust medical model of education and a good career structure with good income potential. The earning opportunity for a podiatrist varies between the type of role and employment base. The NHS uses a grading system called Agenda for Change (AfC), where podiatrists start on Band 5 (sometimes Band 6) and can progress to the highest Band 9. Private practice has no limits and depends on the service offered and skills. Salaries over £100,000 are not unrealistic in successful practices. **David Tollafield**

How did they get into podiatry?

Don't make podiatry your second choice – make it your first choice - podiatrist Jolie Beattie

Podiatry is a career in which a large percentage of people arrive almost by accident. Of course if no one advises you and you do not stumble onto the subject, then it is quite likely you will head for medicine or dentistry, nursing or physiotherapy if you are keen on a healthcare subject. To be fair on the others, the Health & Care Professions Council (HCPC) register covers a wide number of Allied Health Professions (AHPs), not just podiatrists and physiotherapists.

Eleven experiences

These 11 experiences have been selected from lecturers, students and those in clinical practice and describe how they came across podiatry. The most important advice anyone can give to a student still mulling over which career to take is that you are allowed to make a mistake, and many who have shared their story prove change is possible with a good outcome. However, 'experience is simply the name we give to our mistakes,' (*Oscar Wilde*).

Poor career advice

I made some very bad decisions for my 'A' Levels and was given very poor career advice at the age of 16. I took the wrong 'A' Levels, got a car, a boyfriend and a social life. So messed up said 'A' Levels and found myself in clearing. My initial plan was to do a year of podiatry and float myself onto the medicine course. That was all well and good. I got in with my slightly shabby 'A' Level grades. We did the bits with the medics; the anatomy and physiology and we did dissection, and then we did the podiatry specific stuff. We were actually getting our hands on patients within three months. This amazing feeling whilst all the other medics were two years away from that. It's 25 years since I qualified. I still get a buzz out of doing it every day. I still absolutely love it. **Siobhan Muirhead** - *podiatrist*

Foot pain took me to a podiatrist

I started experiencing pain around the bottoms of my feet - my toes were retracted. I didn't really know anything about podiatry at that stage. I was around 22, when I had orthotics made, and it was a whole different side to podiatry, to today, I just needed the hard skin taken off my feet. It was the gait analysis. I thought, I'd really like to go into something like that. I grew to like what she'd done with orthotics made for my feet. I suffered two knee operations through sport, and then I decided I was going to rethink my job. **Paul Haughian** – *student*

Misjudging your ability

I didn't want to be a nurse because I just thought that was hard work and I wasn't bright enough to be a doctor and did not get much help at school to guide my career decision. **Lisa Farndon** - *research podiatrist*

The Colour-blind pilot

When I was young, I wanted to be a pilot. However, it turned out that I was slightly colour blind, and I didn't know that until quite late on at school. I have a slight red/green colour blindness and as a result piloting was out. I really stumbled on podiatry as a career. However, recently I was asked by one of the 4th year students did I ever regret my career choice and not becoming a pilot? My answer was, *"No, not one jot."* I said, *"I've had a fantastic career. It's taken me around the world, lecturing in over 30 countries in my area of diabetic foot disease."* At the end of the day, I did become a pilot as I learned to fly as a private pilot many years later. **Stuart Baird** - *Former Head of School of Podiatry GCU*

No jobs in physiotherapy

Having been a dancer and being injured I started to explore the option of physiotherapy. I went and did lots of work experience in private practice and NHS as well. At the time, all the physios were telling me, don't do it. There's no jobs in physiotherapy - they're getting rid of all the physios. They said, "Go and do podiatry." Of course Jessica Werner did go into podiatry and became a successful business woman. **Jessica Werner** - *podiatrist*

The banner caught my eye!

I was out with my Mum in the car one day, and I noticed a banner with a podiatrist on it advertising a private practice. So then I asked her what a podiatrist did because I'd never seen feet. At that point I was 15 years of age and wanted to play the flute as a professional musician. My mother was actually being treated by a podiatrist so I shadowed her as part of school work experience. Podiatry stood out the most because it was so practical. **Catriona Doyle** – *student*

A Career in Podiatric Medicine

Lightbulb moment

I'd been a very lacklustre mediocre student all my life, certainly in my 'A' Level years at school - but I found that there wasn't much in the way of books, or there wasn't a huge library available to us. But in the books that I did find and started to read, I found that my memory just retained it all. For the first time in my life, I worked and worked intensely at college, laying the foundation for the rest of my career. **Tim Kilmartin** – *consultant podiatric surgeon*

From verruca to Consultant

I had a huge verruca on the underneath of my foot about the size of an old 50 pence piece. My Mum took me to see a podiatrist and he got rid of it completely painlessly. I used to play a lot of sports and still play a bit, so I was interested in sports injuries management, and I was interested in podiatry. So, that's how it all came about. **Ben Yates** – *consultant podiatric surgeon*

Turning IT skills into business podiatry

At the age of 26 I was working as a computer developer and analyst in the NHS and after the birth of my first child decided to rethink my career. An access course boosted my school educational credentials as I did not have the appropriate 'A' Levels. And so I started my career in podiatry as a mother and mature student. **Victoria North** – *independent podiatrist*

Do podiatrists cut toenails?

I was unsure what I wanted to do after leaving school. When visiting my mother where she worked as a ward sister, a senior podiatry manager overheard me ask if a podiatrist just cut toenails! Asked if he could borrow her daughter for the day, I was soon persuaded that there was far more to podiatry than the view that a podiatrist cut toenails. **Jennifer Muir** – *independent podiatrist*

The wrong type of theatre

I had entered the (podiatry) course without the slightest intention of ever practising. I had every intention of following my passion of working in the theatre, not an operating theatre – the real theatre. I would have been on a Stage Management course . But the course was closed one month before my start date. This supported my parents' view that the theatre was unsafe as a career and I should join a profession. So I started at the London Foot Hospital. **Ralph Graham** – *retired consultant podiatric surgeon*

Stepping into a new career

Tales from university students

Student's comments help contribute to the story of podiatry - some are mature, because they came in at a later date than the school leaving age of 18. Many have been in other careers, taken degrees or switched courses. Let's listen to comments from Zoe, Shuja, Ethan, Ellen, Emily, Paul and Paul.

Good mentoring at school
>I was looking at all the healthcare courses on the university website, and podiatry was one that I didn't really know much about, but I looked into it more. There was a podiatrist that goes into my gran, and she was really interesting to talk to. I just happened to be there one day when she was there. I was talking to her and one bit of advice she said to me was 'Stick in with anatomy,' which I have done. **Zoe Alexander** - *Glasgow Caledonian University (GCU)*

Like many, Zoe was unsure what to study when she reached the sixth year in the Scottish system. One teacher gave her the idea that to do any job you needed to love that job and see it as not really going to work. Her teacher took this attitude in her own occupation and this imprinted on the young Zoe.

A Career in Podiatric Medicine

Confusions over title and role

I'm in the third year of the GCU course, I'm just starting to realise all the different aspects of podiatry. Feet are really complex structures, and it's amazing what can go wrong with them. So many people don't know what podiatry is. They often get it mixed up with chiropody or they think it's paediatrics. The podiatrist tries to find out why the callus is building up and relates this to the mechanics of the foot to try to find the cure to prevent it building up again. There's a fair number of underlying problems involved in skin related problems. We are taught how to listen to your patient because they're telling you the diagnosis. The podiatrist needs to solve the problem. And I enjoy doing that. **Zoe Alexander** - *GCU*

The view that the profession deals with cutting toenails and reducing callus can be misleading. Most podiatrists provide medical services and use their skills to find causes, heal wounds and manage pain. The study of skin comes under the general term dermatology.

Making a mistake as your first choice

I was six months into studying audiology and it's you literally hook headphones onto the patient and press a few buttons. And I really thought to myself, *"I'm going to retire at 67. I'm not doing this for the rest of my life. I'm not pressing buttons. I'm not hands on here."* It was a really good life lesson, me knowing myself and what I really wanted to do. At that point I really wanted to do something hands on. **Shuja Merban** - *Huddersfield*

Shuja always knew it was healthcare. She found the idea of caring and compassion important. She wanted to make a difference even if it's small. She studied audiology (another healthcare profession) straight out of sixth form college but, after recognising her wrong turn, she found podiatry.

Placements, high risk and assignments

I liked the patient-people contact at this university. The placements were another key part of the attraction especially in the third year. I enjoy the high-risk side of podiatry and found the subject and module very engaging. I do not enjoy writing up assignments, but actually found podiatric theory modules exciting. I feel more energised than when at school and can embrace my second-year medicine module. **Ethan Clifford** - *Huddersfield*

The Middle-distance runner

I wanted to travel and I knew a few people who went to Glasgow. The course looked very good. A science background is important and plays an important part in subjects like physiology. **Ellen McGeough** - *GCU*

As an 800-metre middle distance runner, Ellen loved anatomy and could relate this to the body. Currently she is interested in common injuries such as Achilles injuries and fasciitis (deeper tears in the sole of the foot). It comes as no surprise that Ellen sees sports podiatry in such a positive light as this is one of the areas her father specialises in as a podiatrist. Ellen selected GCU over her Irish University options.

Anatomy is an important subject
> I definitely would say that the anatomy of the lower limb is where I felt I'd have to target a lot of my extra time outside of lecture times. But with the new language we're learning, and particularly the spelling and pronunciation of some of these words, I felt it's been really difficult. As a first year, anatomy is definitely our hardest subject. There's just so much and it's so new, and it's so detailed. **Emily Reaney** - *Huddersfield University*

Emily suffers from dyslexia. Her tutors provided assistance in regard to any difficulties she experienced. Huddersfield had a warm and welcoming atmosphere and she liked the fact that it had a clinic. Students often fail to understand the importance of the subject of anatomy. It has to be learned, observed and in many cases dissected. Every nerve, blood vessel, ligament and muscle must be memorised in addition to the bones and their sites of attachment.

Attraction to MSK
> I specifically wanted to learn about anatomy and the biomechanics. They've started mentioning parts of physics in the gait and anatomical function modules. I could have got into physiotherapy but I just thought this is more specific to what I want to learn. So that's why I picked it. **Paul Murphy** - GCU

Interprofessional influence
> The hardest part of the course involved the medical side of podiatry. We had a lot of people coming in from the likes of the Royal Hospital or the City, specialists in their field. We were involved with an interprofessional module working alongside physiotherapists doing the group presentations and first aid training. By talking to physios you have an idea about different lower limb cases that they were able to ask you, in the first year.
> **Paul Haughian** - *Ulster*

Podiatry is a three-year full course, except in Scotland where it is four years, leading to a BSc (Hons) degree as the traditional route for school leavers

2- Podiatry is a Medical Subject

Podiatrists are medically trained but are not medical doctors. Learning the language of medical practice is vital. We are called Allied Health Professionals (AHPs). We need to be able to communicate professionally and technically. Since the start of degree courses from the late eighties onwards, the level of science involved in podiatry has increased.

Our actions must follow good medical practice, whether providing medications, arranging an x-ray or blood test, giving a local anaesthetic or making a surgical incision. A podiatrist is a health professional who is passionate about helping people improve their quality of health. Every health professional, in their way, is also an educator.

We have to learn about intricate details, mechanisms and workings of the body from muscles and joints that help the body move, to the organs that make the body function correctly, to preventing disease and helping to reduce pain.

A significant role of the podiatrist is to ensure that the skin is not damaged by pressure, which means having extensive knowledge about footwear, manufacture and design, skin diseases and healing methods.

Learning a new language

Research consists of following scientific methods and translating any findings so that the least educated person can understand – we have to be good communicators. Science embraces the language of Latin, Greek and French words, so we have to make it all sound simple. We are both scientists and communicators, and these skills are interwoven in practice. Anatomy is studied in detail so you need to be aware of dealing with those who have dedicated their bodies to science and learning. Learn why an *'os tibiale externum'* is important to the foot specialist. Be prepared to work with a group of students dissecting a human leg and foot in a medical school. Look at **Table 1** and understand that podiatry is not the study of feet alone. We have to look beyond and consider the whole body. The single most important function of a podiatrist is to screen for foot health concerns and provide advice around the general health of any patient. So let's take this further.

Table 1

Functional elements	Social elements
Blood pressure	Weight gain or loss
Renal & bowel disease	Nutrition
Thyroid & pancreatic function (endocrine)	Alcohol
Cardiac and respiratory efficiency	Smoking
Skin and keratin relationship	Abuse by others
Neuromuscular function and joints	Mental disease and depression
Ability to heal & blood flow	Cancer

Knowing the subject alone is like looking at a skeleton in isolation of its working parts - the organs, muscles, blood flow and nerve innervation. To learn the bones alone makes little sense because then you would not understand how and why the skeleton moves or, in our case, work out why it does NOT move.

> Our course is very medically orientated course. We took a medicine module in the second and third year. I enjoy most of the learning that we do, but the medicine module together with surgery aspect to it and it was looking at X-rays and all the surgical procedures that you can do in the feet. It was really a lot of information at once, so it took a while to get around that. **Judith Watson**

Podiatry looks beyond the foot

Students desire to pass examinations. At university we want students to develop an ability to go beyond the curriculum. Some students wonder why they have to study subjects that seem remote. It is not until you leave university that you realise you require additional information to keep learning and progressing. This also offers you a competitive edge. The degree course has been established to challenge students and provide them with a career for life. Challenge means both developing and creating new thoughts, pushing your ability through learning so that you are equipped with additional knowledge around the subject. University provides the tools for lifelong learning.

Screening

It may surprise many that podiatry is not seen just as looking after feet. We can screen for general health and look for suspicious cancers, swellings, mental health changes, self-harming and domestic abuse. Podiatrists, together with many other AHPs, are the eyes of Primary Medical Care – the family doctor.

The contribution to health care as a multidisciplinary professional is in effect part of a primary care service – the GP. The secondary service exists in the community or hospitals. Surgeons provide tertiary care, the third layer. Their patients do not usually come into a surgery without a letter of referral, unless through A&E which means it might be more urgent.

In the private sector the podiatrist is able to treat from the very young to the not so young. We call this 'cradle to grave' meaning young to old. In the NHS patient categories are not as wide. The image of focusing on age alone mispresents the true worth of the foot health professional.

We deal with anyone who has foot pain or has hurt their foot or ankle, to those who have broken a foot bone or have injuries through skiing or other sports activities. We deal with people who are sick or have suffered mental or developmental problems. We give advice to help healthy people remain healthy. We look after older patients where walking is important to retain their independence.

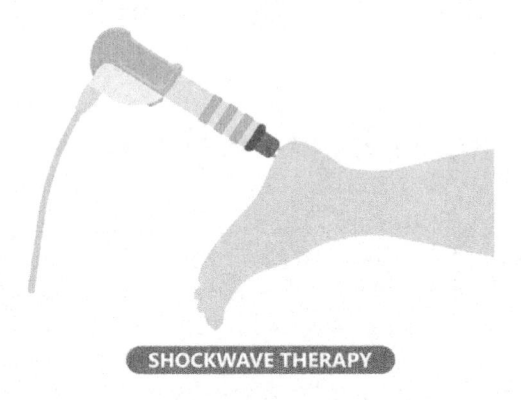

SHOCKWAVE THERAPY

Pain is at the heart of what we manage, and over the last half-century, new techniques have come along to offer a wide range of treatments without the need for certain medicines. The podiatrist uses many electronic and treatment devices at their disposal, from laser to ultrasound, cryotherapy to extracorporeal shock wave (illustrated), and transcutaneous nerve stimulators (TNS) to radiofrequency methods.

Of course, many desire to undertake surgery and with local anaesthetic, as in dentistry, perform minor operations. Bone and joint surgery falls outside the undergraduate course – but you will see surgery being performed on all parts of the foot by podiatrists with extended training.

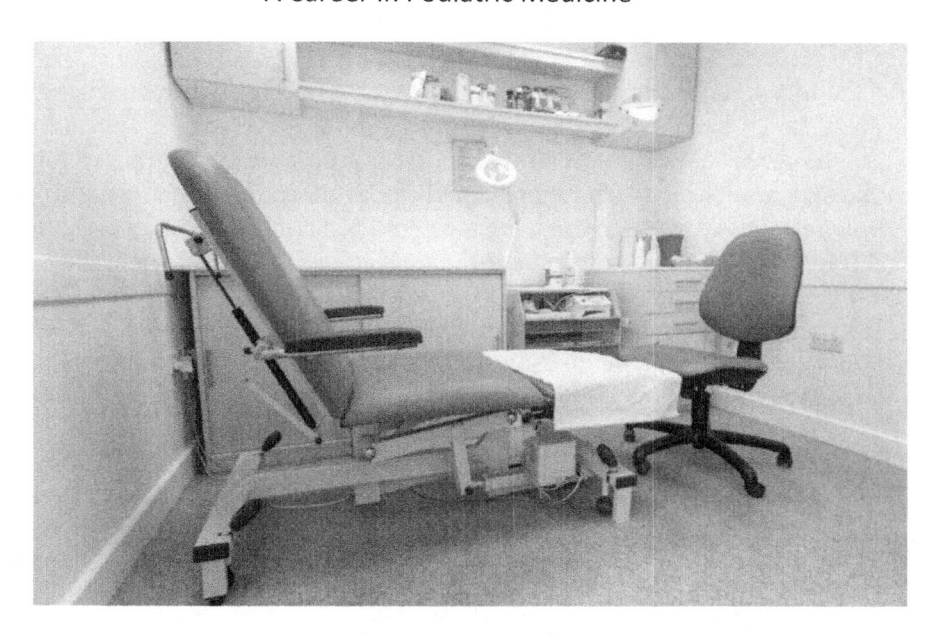

A modern podiatry practice may appear to look like a dental clinic. C/O Debbie Delves. 2022

Working in clinical practice

Most podiatrists want to treat people, others teach or focus on research. This is a multifaceted profession with a wide variety of opportunities.

Of course, if you prefer, you can work part-time to suit your family, but you must keep up your practice hours to retain your registration and Continuous Professional Development (CPD). It is unlikely as a young podiatrist you would work part-time, but for mature students this has considerable appeal.

Registration

Once qualified you need to register to practice in the UK as a podiatrist. Registration is renewed every two years through the Health and Care Professional Council (HCPC). You are required to be registered (licensed) to practice as a podiatrist forming the body known as AHPs.

You cannot access medicines, work in the NHS, or practice as a podiatrist unless you are registered.

Face-to-face contact offers a variety of opportunities, and for the most part, people are decent and want to follow your advice, others are more resistant so you learn to work around the problem. Employment within the NHS takes place in a health centre or hospital department, or you can set up your practice and equip it, or work in an established firm of podiatrists – often formed into a limited company.

House calls take you into homes, known as 'domiciliary,' which allows you to examine patients in their own environment. Some podiatrists like working in retirement homes - supporting care workers and nursing staff.

Unlike the USA, the UK armed forces has no dedicated career structure or ranking for the profession. To work in the medical corps and attain a rank in the British army, one would have to join up without the guarantee of using your skills. That said, you would, in all probability, gain from new skills having a medical background. Podiatrists still provide care for our armed services in their practices.

Working in independent hospitals has grown in the last 30 years. e.g. Nuffield, Ramsay, Spire, to name a few. Podiatrists work with physiotherapists and provide a comprehensive musculoskeletal (MSK) support service. This is available in both the NHS and independent sector.

There are payment schemes for podiatric treatment outside the NHS, and some insurers now reimburse a limited list of treatments.

While the independent sector has wider freedom, the NHS service has focused on 'At-Risk' categories rather than delivering generalist care. At-risk is a term commonly used for any patient who under normal circumstances would heal or fight off infection easily, but might not do so easily if a medical condition existed. Different working patterns are discussed in detail in **Section 4.**

Sarah feels she has tremendous support from the NHS and is well supported. She emphasises though the major difference between the NHS and independent sector is the fact the department has to focus on risk across the spectrum of patients. The same patients are still seen as they always have, the young and elderly, but that focus is based around an association with risk.

NHS Supporting Knowledge & development

You have the opportunity to go on study days and go onto courses and get into the acute sector because podiatry is mainly in the community. I've also been lucky enough to be part of the nail surgery team as a Band 6 and do that once or twice a week from start to finish. It's just so satisfying! We focus on the disease process, on how to manage patients and how to give them the best care. And again, it's all about preventing these problems, preventing them losing a limb, preventing them losing a digit, preventing them losing their life because of their poor health. **Sarah Twiss** - *NHS Podiatrist*

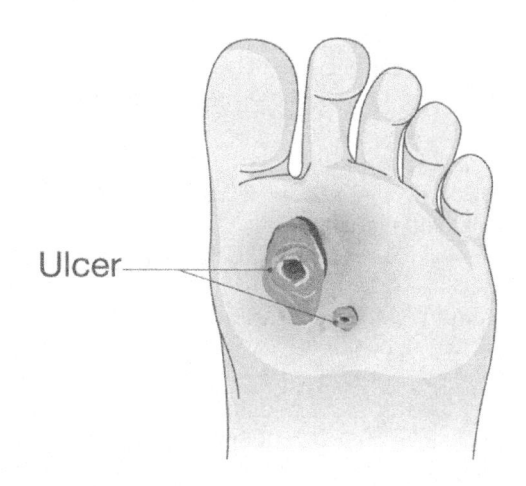

The ulcer is mentioned constantly through this book. It is any break in the skin, and our concern is one where the wound doesn't heal

Sarah rotates around six clinics. A lot of Band 5 work is seeing routine patients. Short recall is where somebody has previously had an ulcer or is at high-risk of a breakdown due to their skin and loss of tissue viability, reduced vascular status or deteriorating health, and Sarah's team monitors them closely. They are advised about smoking, diet, exercise, maintaining the feet in good order and checking their footwear from damage.

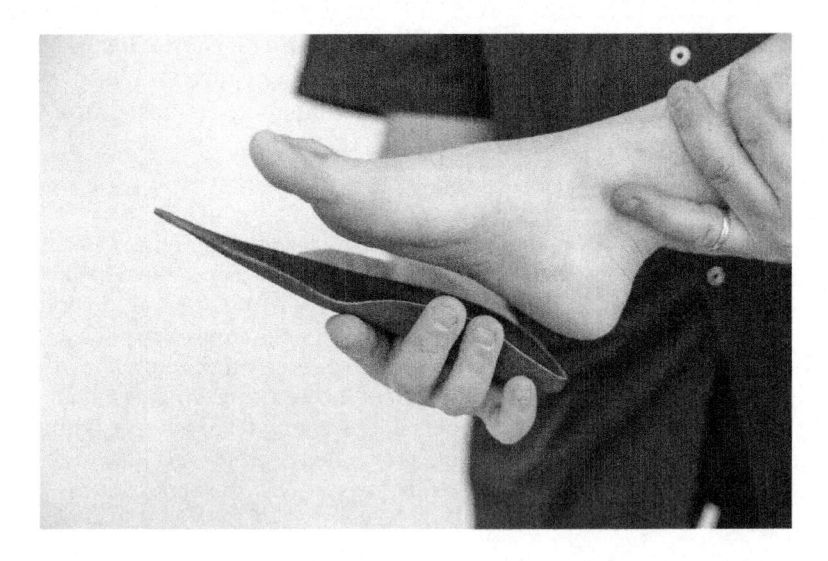

The use of orthoses (orthotics) is an important part of how we manage patient pressures under the foot. This helps to take away or off-load the type of forces that cause damage to the skin

Not all NHS Trusts have an orthotic lab.
> In our high-risk foot clinic, we see those patients with an active ulceration that we're managing with orthotics. So we manage it in the department. We use offloading insoles and modified shoes, and once they're healed we make sure they're in a decent shoe and allocated an appointment on the short recall clinic to monitor progress. We have our own orthotics lab. We're one of the few NHS Trusts that still has that and we make our own orthotics. We don't have a technician there. We do have a fantastic MSK podiatrist who is brilliant. He supports us all through the orthosis making and gives us a lot of training. It's a really good service to have, and it's one that we're going to definitely keep on fighting to keep the service. **Sarah Twiss**

Within the last few years the shortage of podiatrists in the NHS has given way to a new focus in using a group called Foot Health Practitioners. You can never remove politics from any profession and some see FHPs as intrusive to their earning capacity. The truth is that FHPs form part of a new workforce.

Advancing your clinical career

We have seen, up to Band (Agenda for Change) AfC 6, that one can still specialise within the NHS, but climbing further requires more in-house training and taking on further educational development. Hospitals offer specialised care in diabetes, rheumatology (medicine), and orthopaedics (trauma & surgery). The idea is to keep patients in the community but maintain their independence.

Multidisciplinary Teams (MDT) have been established to offer a comprehensive and rapid service for those waiting to see consultants. Podiatrists and physiotherapists now triage (filter) patients, so they don't have to wait to see a consultant. This is part of secondary care. The general podiatrist or GP might refer into an MDT.

Treatment can be provided by Extended Scope Practitioners (ESPs) on higher salaries (AfC 7-8). They undertake work previously performed by a consultant or doctor; injections and tests can be conducted swiftly. If patients require foot surgery by a consultant (orthopaedic or podiatric) surgeon, a referral is tailored to that requirement.

Such integration has made podiatry exciting but opens the career to more opportunities—other ESPs work within the framework of medical departments, mainly diabetes and vascular surgery or rheumatology. The latter specialty caters for joints and muscle pain related to autoimmune disease but with the aim to establish mobility.

There are two relatively new categories of specialism, while not so new elsewhere in healthcare they are being adopted by the podiatry profession; Advanced Clinical Practitioner (ACP) and First Contact Practitioner. **Karl Guttormsen** reports on ACP later on.

Other developing areas

These include dermatology medicine, pain management and A&E. At the time of publication no formal role has been created for the podiatrist as part of a primary A&E team although secondary referrals may be made back to podiatry.

The foot and lower limb are susceptible to injury and disease. Having a healthy blood supply to the limb is not the only concern. Most podiatrists act as 'physicians' of the feet, using new techniques such as dermoscopy (a specialised magnifying glass) to alert specialists and GPs to potential foot cancers. For example, melanoma (pigmented mole) shortens lives and can be spotted on feet. In addition, nails often have hidden cancers lying below them. Nail management is not about beautifying the foot but recognising disease. Podiatrists may be the first to spot these changes. Podiatrists work with cancer patients because cancer treatment affects the feet (see *Afni Shah-Hamilton*).

Several colleagues sought overseas opportunities and upon returning to the UK have brought their new skills back to the health care system and progressed their career development. There is never a better time to participate in such programmes than while you are young.

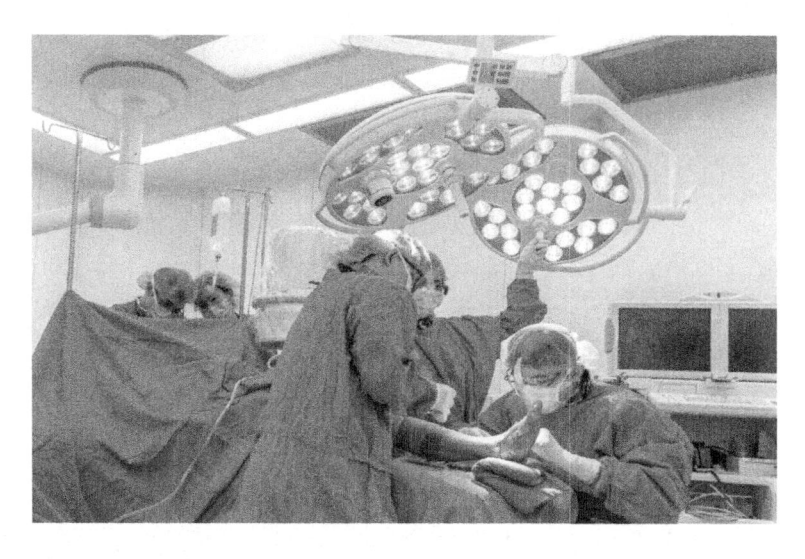

Podiatrists operate in real operating theatres after extended training

Postgraduate training in surgery

One of the most developed parts of podiatry is a career in the area of surgery within the NHS. The call to a surgical career is long, intensive and expensive but highly rewarding. Usamah Khalid explains a little about his journey so far.

The BSc (Hons) Podiatry programme is a pre-requisite for any progression into Podiatric Surgery.

> Training for podiatric surgery typically involves the completion of the MSc in The Theory of Podiatric Surgery which is a pre-requisite. Thereafter, a surgical passport will need to be completed before beginning your three-year practical training which is awarded by competitive interview.
>
> Part One, Two and Three are completed each year before fully qualifying. Training from undergraduate to qualified surgeon can take between seven and nine years. The main difference between undergraduate and postgraduate study is making your whole patient appraisal stronger to stand up to the higher level of responsibilities honed across your career.
>
> Podiatric Surgery is an exciting specialism of podiatry, combining

multiple strands of specialisms to perform complex foot and ankle surgery to correct a patient's pain/deformity. It goes one step further of managing mechanical complaints by conservative care and allows you to properly intervene to improve that patient's quality of life. There is the added benefit of combining knowledge and skill with manual dexterity.

The podiatric surgeon heads a team at consultant level providing tertiary care. Working with anaesthetists and nurses forms an integrated team, with many centres offering a trainee programme for podiatry graduates.

A *surgical passport* is a short contract and essential to ensure a candidate wishing to undertake surgery has exposure to a surgical programme. As part of this formal placement, the candidate is also assessed. This provides a two-way process so that everyone can be assured that the candidate should go forwards to surgical training which could take a further three years, which means the long period of investment is assured. He or she embraces all the knowledge of an undergraduate but assumes the responsibilities of a medical surgeon adopting the role of postgraduate mentor and dealing with foot deformities and minor trauma. In addition, sub-specialities have arisen in diabetic foot preservation, where patients are at high-risk but benefit from surgery. Further discussion on surgery can be found in **Section 5.**

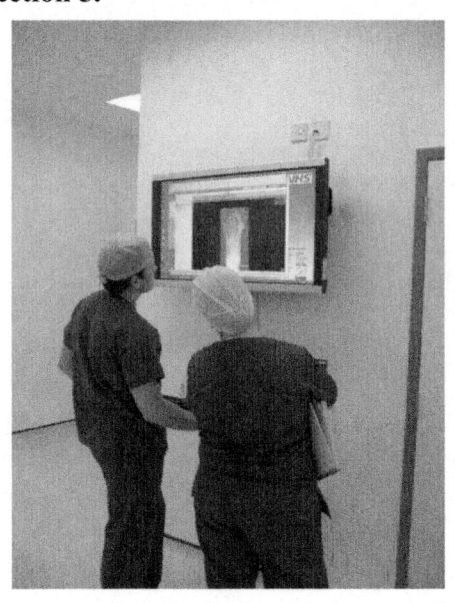

The image below shows a trainee podiatric surgeon (left) talking to third year placement student (University of Wolverhampton).

Opportunities outside the NHS
Industrial consultancy

What is industrial or commercial podiatry? Perhaps we can use the term for any activity where one is not employed as part of an NHS or independent practice. This would exclude those who rent or use services from other locations. Locum work usually comes from an agency and this is where industrial working might commence. There is no set reference.

> Following engagement by an independent healthcare provider to the *Highways Agency*, I was approached to advise on safety footwear. Officers who had foot problems were unable to cope with the standard boot issued. After examining and reporting on the first six officers, I found myself not only examining over 35 officers but had to travel to the southwest office in Bristol. The consultancy was supposed to last six months but ended up taking a year. **David Tollafield**

One could be employed by a chain of shops (*see Claire Carr*), a prison service (*see Jonathan Small*) or a firm keen to expand health to its employees. Sometimes podiatrists are best to approach different outlets directly to offer their services. This could include football clubs and dance studios. Opportunities have opened up in the areas of sportswear, protection against blisters (see *Mike McColgan*), and safety footwear.

Orthoses

Podiatry is unique among other professions. As well as learning about the theory of podiatric medicine and surgery, students are taught many practical skills, including how to manufacture a range of products for foot conditions. This ranges from orthoses (orthotics) to prostheses. In addition, knowledge of manufacturing and material sciences is invaluable and taught with mechanical therapeutics. However, the term mechanical therapy may not be used by all schools of podiatry.

Two examples of enterprise from the 1980s:
>Antony P Barcroft set up Langer (UK) in the 1980s to provide a quality prescription device service for podiatrists. In contrast, Clive Over set up OVA instruments, using his knowledge as a podiatrist to supply his profession with surgical instruments and clinical products. Independent podiatrists are ever more creative, demonstrating that their skills can be transferred to other avenues, something that Tony Gavin did, having left the commercial world and entering podiatry only to form OSGO as part of the independent support service for podiatrists. These actions come under innovation.

Legal & helping the Courts

>The author Peter James writes a crime series around a character called DCI Roy Grace. Within the storyline, Haydn Kelly (a real podiatrist) appears as the forensic podiatrist helping the Brighton police solve crimes in *'Dead Man's Time'* and *'Not Dead Yet.'*

The legal side of podiatry has grown with expert witness work assisting injured parties to follow claims by supporting lawyers and barristers (*see Barry Francis & Wes Vernon*).

>Podiatrists specialising in forensic science and practice do not just help the police but also the courts, using their knowledge of foot type, the relationship between feet and shoes, clinical records and the different patterns associated with walking. The study of walking, or gait, is taught to all students at university using sophisticated electronic equipment that many will introduce into their practices. **Wes Vernon**

Business Coaching and Authorship

Podiatrists have found other avenues to use their skills and widen their role, which runs in parallel with their professional aspirations. Supporting podiatry practices with their business development is fairly new and growing. A few podiatrists have also taken to writing books – some fictional, others contribute to the library of material for podiatry. There is no blueprint for what is seen as a career model and new opportunities can be found with a little ingenuity and looking for a gap in the market.

Royal College of Podiatry

Over the years the Royal College of Podiatry has advertised 'professional roles' within the organisation with the profession advising members on a wide range of activities. This type of employment does require a number of years in the field of practice.

The effect of Covid-19 on podiatry

We do not have enough UK medical doctors in general practice, and the pandemic has emphasised this weakness. Podiatrists stepped up in many centres as vaccinators during the 'pandemic,' while others worked to help patients recover or to ease waiting times.

Podiatry has grown because of these openings and because it is a profession that does not believe in stagnating and knows it can expand.

Feet are the barometers of health and often fail to have the care they deserve; health care delivery is no longer solely GP-focused. As a result, the chances of podiatrists taking on more responsibility are ever on the cards with the introduction of *First Contact Practitioners* and *Advanced Clinical Podiatrists*.

The future is exciting and challenging. But, above all else, this profession is going places and is worth looking at. Podiatrist Stephanie Owen says, *'changing lives matter.'* Feet form the link between the ground and the moving body above the foot.

Job availability in podiatry
Demand and Opportunity

While England probably appears to have wider opportunities, the other UK nations have plenty of opportunities available for the creative practitioner. One of the changes in recent years has been the expansion of independent practices taking on graduates and employees. Raymond Robinson and Stuart Baird offer opinions from Northern Ireland and Scotland.

> The Department of Health are pushing diabetes and wound care a lot more. Staff have been moved into more senior positions to fill those posts, creating a shortage of Band 5 posts. There's also a big demand in private practice. I'm inundated with emails around this time of year from private practitioners looking for student graduates for part-time or full-time employment. Student podiatrists have made a very good choice of career because there's never been a better time to join our profession. There's tons of work out there. They have their pick of jobs to some degree. Whereas, when I started, it wasn't like that.
> **Raymond Robinson** - *Head of School, Ulster University*

> The diversity of podiatry in Scotland is considerable, and potentially suits all tastes and different aspirations. If you want to work in a rural setting you could go to Stornoway, a small town in the Outer Hebrides, a group of islands on the west coast of Scotland. To carry out a home visit you might have to take your car to a small ferry, then go by boat, and finally arrive at the patient's house by another car. However, big cities still have a certain lure and I know several of my ex-students over the past few years are now working in Guys and St Thomas' Hospitals or Primary Care Trusts in London. There is an attraction of the big smoke that still draws graduates away from Scotland. Regardless of where you practice or the job you carry out all aspects of podiatry should require you to practice at the top of your license utilising and developing the skills you acquired during your undergraduate education. **Stuart Baird** - *Former Head of School of Podiatry, GCU*

The NHS Podiatrist

That first decision
> It was always my belief that I needed the experience of colleagues who could help me over my initial period following graduation. Understanding the NHS and it structures allowed this before stepping out. Within three years I felt confident enough to step into private practice. **David Tollafield**

If you choose to enter the NHS you will do so on a Band that equates to your graduate experience.

> You start as a Band 5 at the bottom of a signpost almost, and as you climb up the signpost as a Band 6 you get all these little edges off. And then I think once you choose an edge to go off, that's when you focus on your Band 7 roles, but spend as much time as a Band 6 as you can to really focus on which direction you want to go in. **Sarah Twiss**

Sarah worked in one location for 18 months then moved to a second NHS Trust picking up a Band AfC6. She trained at the Birmingham School of Podiatry (University of Wolverhampton).

Contrasting AfC Band 5 with Band 6

I got a really good education as a Band 5. I was very, very lucky. I got to shadow some very good podiatrists. We do a lot of the routine care. We look after people's feet where they do need NHS intervention, but they're not quite up to that point where we're seeing them every week, and we're debriding wounds and things like that. It's very much the preventative part of podiatry and learning around how to prevent problems occurring in the future that would need people to come and see them also.

Luckily I had the opportunity to band up to a Band 6. I love the Band 6 role because I get to have a little bit more autonomy. I have a little bit more responsibility, which is always quite nice, and you get to really focus on the area that you want to stay in. I think that was the big difference for me as I was very much diabetes, diabetes all the way through university, all the way through my Band 5, 18 months. My focus has switched to vascular because as a Band 6 having that opportunity to again shadow different services and work more autonomously with more poorly patients and see more disease processes at a more advanced stage, has really shifted to what I really enjoy. **Sarah Twiss**

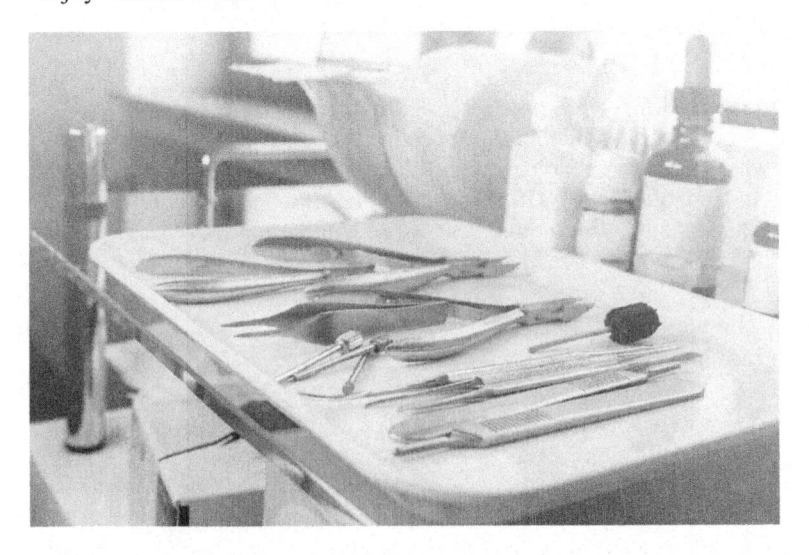

All podiatry instruments are sterilised before use and comprise anything from specialist implements to examine the skin and nails, through to wound packs and surgical instruments separately prepared in hospitals

University is not just about going to a big institution to learn, but to acquire a life-long skill, make friends and build your network to influence your career

3- Studying Podiatry at University: *The nuts & bolts*

Let's assume you have selected podiatric medicine as your chosen career - you will want to know as much as possible about what to expect. If you are at that point of selecting GCSE subjects then you will find the next section valuable as BSc degree students talk about their experiences based on interviews when they were at university.

You will learn about what material is taught, when you first get to see patients, and gain advice from students and staff experiences and thoughts. The biggest attraction is early patient contact and placements.

Selecting a university in the United Kingdom

The bullet points summarise the key forms of entry.

- Direct from school to university 'A' Levels 18 years of age
- Access course after graduating from another occupation 18+
- Newer entry mechanisms for mature entry with appropriate qualification 18+

There are currently thirteen universities representing podiatry degree courses in the United Kingdom (see map).

English universities –

Brighton (Eastbourne)	South East coast
Plymouth	South West coast
Huddersfield	North central
Southampton	South coast
Durham	North East

London UCL, which originally had two centres (London Foot Hospital and Chelsea based at Paddington)

Northampton	East Midlands
Birmingham (Wolverhampton)	West Midlands
Manchester (Salford)	North West

Northern Ireland –

Ulster

Wales –

Cardiff Metropolitan

Scotland –

Glasgow Caledonian University
Queen Margaret University, Edinburgh

A Career in Podiatric Medicine

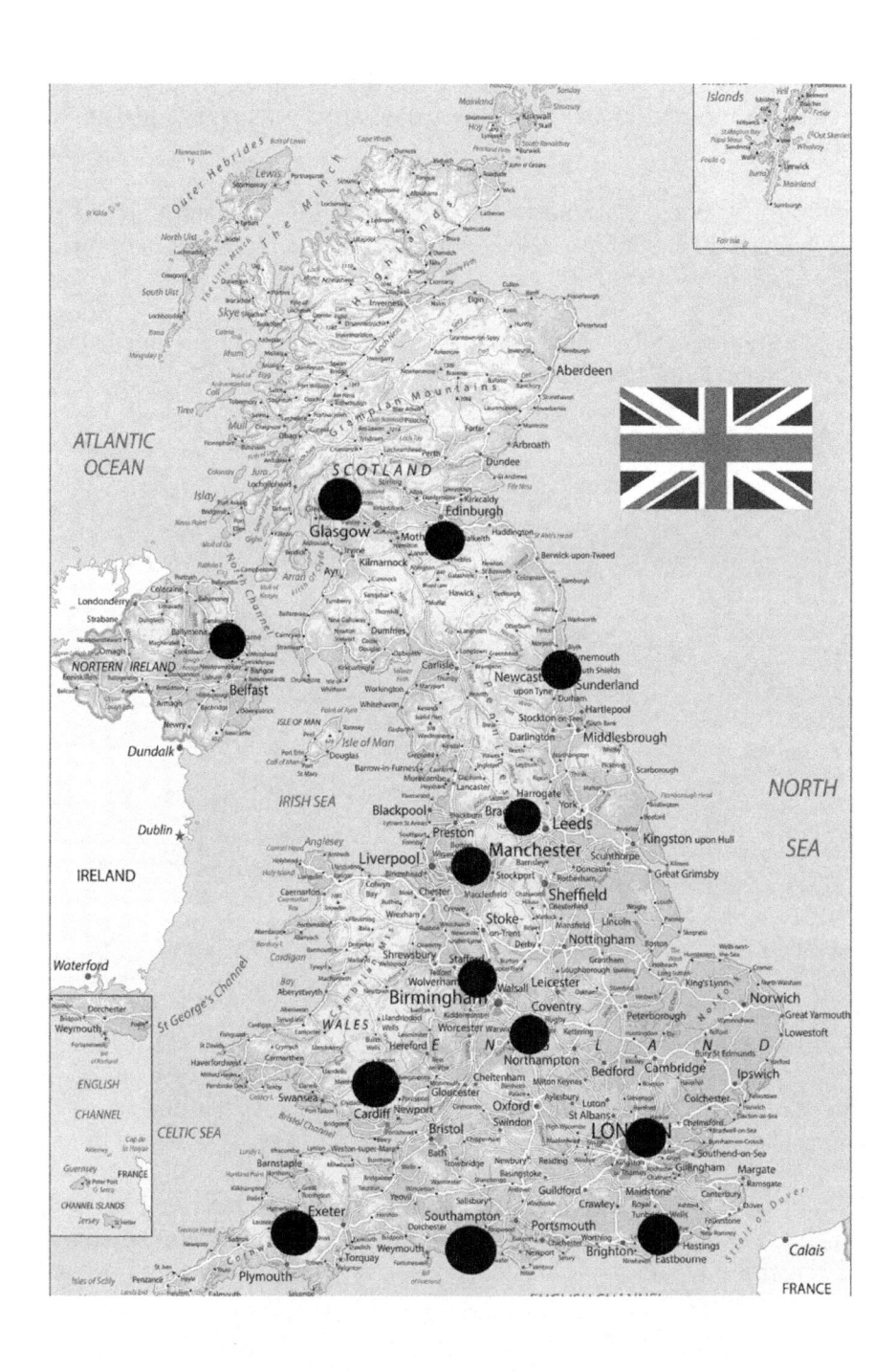

Terms used

'School of Podiatry' is the older name for the institution of podiatry but maybe also referred to as a 'College of Podiatry,' a term favoured in the past.

Within this book, 'schools' and 'colleges' of podiatry are used interchangeably and therefore may appear in the same context but remain part of Schools of Health Sciences.

Courses are frequently shared with other health courses including medical and dental students, providing lectures covering similar material.

Avoid choosing the wrong career path

It is difficult for any student to know what the long corridor of life brings. Still, careers teachers and those in universities bear some responsibility in understanding that courses often do not turn out to be what a student needs or indeed wants.

We will meet a few examples of wrong turns from other courses into podiatry. Equally, some students find podiatry is not right and hopefully this career guide will provide enough information to minimise any errors in decision making.

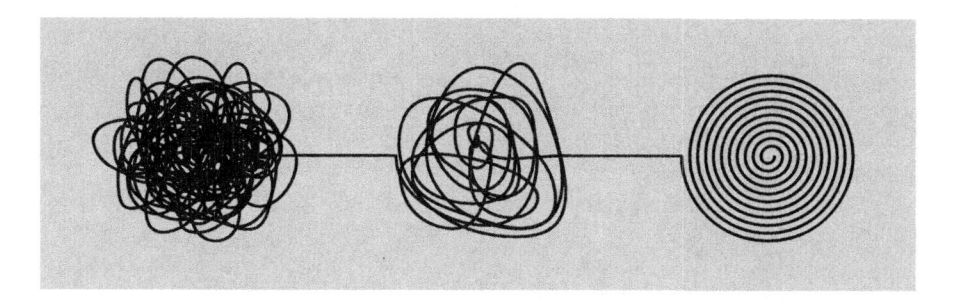

Transforming from school to university

Many students find the change from school or sixth form college challenging when entering university. There is a change in style. Teaching is different to lecturing although, by A level, the style of teaching and studying will have changed from GCSE.

Teaching tends to ensure certain facts are presented. Lecturing presents facts in a broad sense. Think of a cupboard with coat hangers. The hangers are essential for those clothes. However, you have to decide how many clothes and the types of clothes you wish to stock in your wardrobe. Lecturing is like the wardrobe – you will have the essentials but you are expected to read around the subject. How much effort you put in equals the benefit you receive. The more clothes you have the wider your choice. Expanding your range of subject matter requires discipline and knowledge using libraries and search engines. Given the internet and integration with computer skills, most school leavers adjust quickly. Mature students can find buckling down to studying and IT methods challenging.

With a wide range of guided materials on offer to help students, universities have plenty of resources to help those who have left home maybe for the first time, cope. Older prejudices, which have long been recognised with respect to dyslexia, are now seen as a positive attribute rather than negative. Some students prefer to live at home but to engage in a full student experience. Nothing beats the sense of independence and even though I qualified over 40 years ago; that sense of taking responsibility and having freedom was something I enjoyed, and one which my own children also found. The attraction of clubs, making new friends, and finding you are free from the discipline of home-family life can take getting used to.

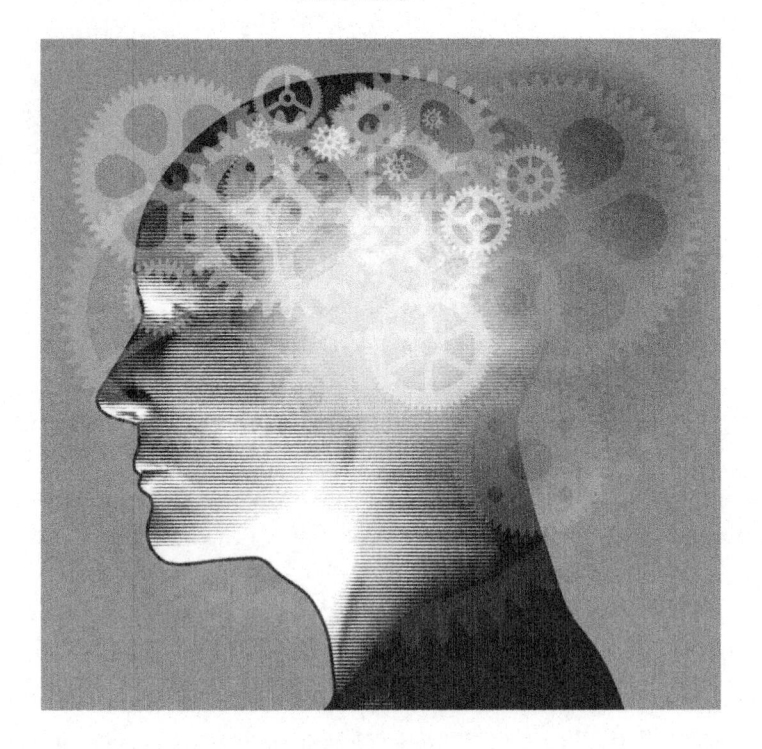

We all require time to assess our experiences and learn to make adjustments for our future

Reflective thoughts from podiatry students

Students are advised to attend open days, read the university prospectus and generally ensure they get out and about by observing NHS and private clinics to form a wide impression of the potential landscape.

What core podiatry is
>It's not about cutting nails and stuff, especially in this last year now with the third years. When we do NHS patients, it's normally high risk or nail surgery. It's really dealing with skin and pressure that cause chronic problems. **Ryan Brain**

Pick the sciences
>I would very much recommend picking all three sciences - chemistry, biology, and physics, but also pick art subjects because for insole making - it's good because you're kind of using both sides of your brain, so you're using the right and the left in different spheres of

A Career in Podiatric Medicine

your brain. **Ektaa Vadgama**

Using communication skills

You build on communication skills, which I think is an invaluable skill to have in podiatry. I think when people think of podiatry, they just think of nails, whereas there's many more areas that make this only contribute to a small amount of the role of a podiatrist. **Ellen McGeough**

Incorporating medicine

Podiatry is multifaceted (has lots of different graduate routes to take). There's a slice of medicine, it could be dermatology, or musculoskeletal, wound care, and the high-risk foot. Feet are a real window to your health. **Emily Reaney**

Choice

There's so many different sub areas you can go into. I think generally the career opportunities are really quite vast and there's so many areas you can go into. I think that's definitely another really big appeal. **Ethan Clifford**

A future in wound care

I'm trying to do diabetic wounds. When a wound starts healing, you can actually see the changes. I just like the challenge. It's quite a highly skilled job, that's for sure. **Ryan Brain**

Studying away from class

I think I did make some changes, mostly setting aside more time for studying. For example, when I was at school I would just do my homework and that would be it, whereas at university we have to study and set aside more time. In the first and second years, we were in university most of the time. My class was quite small; there were only 26 of us. So we had groups set up, but I could never do any studying in the study groups. So I prefer studying by myself. I don't know. I just get distracted too easily. **Zoe Alexander**

Mature students

Later on we see how graduates develop their careers over the years, emphasising the breadth of podiatric practice. Some are mature students at entry, some already have families and some come to the university from another country where their mother tongue is not English.

Entering the profession from outside the UK, or coping with a family while studying, shows how much people are prepared to juggle their lives. Younger students may find such disparity of age strange at first, but soon learn not only to adjust but embrace the experience of having mature students in class. Paul Murphy is married and admits it's difficult at age 40 with children.

> If I'm taking the kids to school, picking them up, and taking them to their classes after school, this is a challenge with my studies. **Paul Murphy** (Student)

Students have to undertake directed reading which means expanding their knowledge by self-discovery. Universities provided extensive library resources

Reading Podiatric Medicine

Students applying for podiatry might wonder why it takes so long to study feet. Feet belong on the legs upon which movement depends for efficiency and smooth movement. This we call gait, the walking cycle comparing contact and swing.

The body has a system of nerves and blood to supply every cell, tissue, joint, muscle, and skin. The heart, lungs, brain and central nervous system must be intact and functioning to maintain oxygen for movement. The kidneys, liver, thyroid and pancreas maintain much of the body's systems homeostasis through a balance of minerals, vitamins, and hormones, providing nutrients and removing waste. The alimentary system acquires nutrients to energise the body, but must also extract content not required. (*See – you need biology to understand these terms alone!*)

The foot is one of the body's barometers for disease, none more so than nail colour, shape and quality. The skin provides another barometer for nutritional assessment and is the first of the connective tissues to be visibly examined from the face to the hands and feet.

For the clinician studying medicine and physiology, feet hold a carrier bag full of opportunities to view the healthy human. Patients have told me on occasions that GPs have been known to scribble a prescription for medication for their feet without them even removing their shoes!

Hopefully, as you read the different clinical comments, you will appreciate that the substance of podiatry as a career is far from drab and contains significant challenges for the enquiring mind.

The degree is based on 'podiatric medicine' because the curriculum covers much that a medical doctor must know and, in many cases, more than a doctor will ever know about feet. It is only after doctors study orthopaedics that they expand their knowledge of feet, mechanics (biomechanics) and pathology.

Studying orthopaedics requires extended medical training. Therefore, doctors at medical school going into general practice often have limited exposure because other areas of medicine are prioritised. Podiatry is not the same as orthopaedics, but a substantial section of podiatric medicine relies on orthopaedic knowledge. Our interest in skin and wound healing, knowledge of footwear and orthoses is greater than orthopaedics, but the two professions share close associations.

Students will find biology a useful science, but there are other subjects of value

The Importance of Science in Podiatry on Entry

Each university course will set its own entry requirements and emphasise the subjects they wish you to have. A shortage of podiatry exists in the main sectors – NHS and independent practice. The independent sector includes the private self-paying sector but may absorb contract work from the NHS.

Interviews may require candidates to undertake a presentation, offering good reasons why they would wish to take up podiatry. Therefore, preparing your answer before your visit makes sense. Read up (*hence my book*), visit a practice in the NHS and independent sector, and research the subject. You can also find - *Foot Health Myths, Facts & Fables (AMAZON)* useful in giving a preview of many foot conditions, thus helping to understand what contributes to a podiatrist's workload.

Biology, chemistry, and physics are strong entry subjects, but mixing other subjects can still be valuable. Many students find chemistry and physics can be picked up within the course but find the concepts challenging without a scientific background. Biology at 'A' Level is near enough mandatory. Physics helps understand the science behind the principles of muscle function, human movement and various technical equipment used in podiatry. As Benjamin Jones (*University of Southampton*) points out –

> Every application is also based on context – if one has taken action by selecting a different subject, such as sports science at A 'level, this can make a difference to your application.

Alongside science, art and craft make good partners as podiatry is practical – requiring good hand-eye coordination (psycho-motor skills). Unlike dentistry, medicine and veterinary science, grades are not always onerous. Good communication requires a decent handle on languages, English being the primary language as the course and references are in English. Parallel languages from Asia, the Middle East (Arabic) and Europe are highly beneficial as many patients in the UK come from different ethnic groups.

> I took biology, English language and art, which might seem like quite a bizarre range of things. Still, I thought, well, biology, I'm choosing that because I definitely want to work in healthcare and for that I'm going to have to understand how the body works and everything else. Art, I'm quite a creative person - it was something that I knew I would enjoy, and I knew that I would do well in and English as well. It was another thing I just really enjoyed. People always think that's a bizarre combination, but that was enough to get me a place. **Shona Wesley**

Selecting biology, chemistry, P.E, English, Maths, and Business -

> It's good to have a good grounding, but when you get into the first year, you go through it again. But if you haven't done that in school, then you're at more of a disadvantage, I would say, because you haven't already learnt it before. **Zoe Alexander**

As business management is an integral part of clinical practice, taking a business course is highly relevant, but most university courses do not have time to build a specific business and management module into the undergraduate course. Understanding budgets and efficiencies are highly applicable in management. (*See Suzy Taylor* and how she managed economics in the NHS)

Further discussion on the business side of practice is described by several podiatrists who run multi-disciplinary and multi-clinic practices in **Section 4**.

While we encourage a relaxed style to patient interviews with patients, uniforms are used in schools of podiatry to protect clothes and appear professional

Defining Clinical Skills
Early patient contact

Having an idea of the course structure will offer an appreciation of the direction of study. First and second years in formal medicine cover medical sciences, anatomy, physiology, pathology and pharmacology before starting on the clinical sciences. Podiatry is unique in that most students follow the medical model up to a point but embark on clinical studies within the first year as well as patient contact.

Treatment programmes cover health conditions around parallel subjects which overlap with elements of sociology and psychology. Both subjects are not taught formally, not because the subjects are unimportant, but fitting such broad material is difficult to slot in. Students must learn how to manage pain, undertake a range of diagnostic tests and some school courses cover independent (private practice and business). These are softer subjects and students should seek out their own study regarding the latter by visiting private practices that have a strong business model. Examples are provided in the **Section 4**. For some, looking at a list of subjects may not mean much, so more descriptive detail will follow and should be beneficial when we reach some of our student experiences.

Psycho-Motor (PSM) learning

Building motor skills requires dexterity and delicate movements. Learning to use sharp instruments and not damage deeper structures beneath the skin and the nail bed are explicitly developed. The second element of this skill is carrying out these actions without causing repetitive strain to the hand and not damaging patients with sharp instruments.

As keratin tissue – the top layer of the skin thickens - students must, at the outset, be able to 'debride' the keratin accurately and navigate blood vessels. Debridement is the process of removing dead and decaying tissue. It may sound repugnant, but this is the basis behind building our primary surgical skills - whether in general surgery, veterinary or dental practice.

Cantilever nippers allow efficient mechanical advantage and strength and are capable of cutting through bone and hard tissue

The PSM skill must be conducted with efficient speed without damaging the operator. No one needs to be told that scalpels are sharp and this author has indeed cut himself as a student with gratifying spurts of the red stuff. A pair of modern cantilever nippers can cut through bone, let alone skin, with moderate ease, and so you have to manipulate such instruments with the same care as scalpels.

A Career in Podiatric Medicine

By the time a student graduates, precision and speed are often admired by the most senior consultant in medicine, not least because scalpel work can be conducted without anaesthetic. Moreover, those who go on to deal with vascular-deprived (ischaemic) ulcers can do so with consummate skill, a skill which commences in the first year of the podiatry course. Ben Yates, and Martin Fox honed their skills when dealing with their overseas leprosy experience.

Podiatrists who become foot surgeons can use these primary skills with greater precision, something even the most qualified medical surgeons do not possess before starting their surgical career. Therefore, skills developed when an undergraduate student can be used to build upon during the life of one's occupation.

Clinical skills in medicine or any clinical health-led subject must be delivered safely and with the patient's welfare in mind. The legal aspects of clinical work are essential and can cover patient data protection, health & safety, communications skills, and consent. Clinical record-keeping now plays a large part in recording any communication between clinician and patient. With increased medical litigation, no podiatrist wants to fall to the prey of an army of lawyers looking for a quick buck for their patients and a larger payout for their services supplied on a no win no fee system! You will meet Barry Francis in **Section 4** as he talks about the legal process under expert witness podiatry.

All students will understand the difference between a developing child's foot, a typical adult foot, high-risk foot diseases, and sports injuries. In addition, many patients have mental health conditions and dealing with the wide variety of patient personalities is not easily taught without many hours of clinical exposure.

As patients age, we see problems of mobility and falls where conditions become more typical to the process of age, stiffness and deformity. Australian podiatry professor, Hylton B Menz, La Trobe University, has made it his life's work to study the older patient and conditions upon which much undergraduate study is based. Such pantheons of podiatric academia are changing the face and landscape of modern podiatry with exciting offshoots.

Musculoskeletal or MSK podiatry is not a specialist subject. It requires a strong foundation in biomechanics to understand human movement, physiology and pathology of connective tissues. Many podiatrists still talk about biomechanics as some advanced study and indeed there are courses set up for qualified podiatrists to look at this field. However, like anatomy, all podiatrists must apply some elements of MSK principles to all of their clinical work.

A biomechanical examination is an orthopaedic/podiatric examination of the musculoskeletal system. A biomechanical profile may entail electromyography, force-pressure measurement and studying the angular changes of the body framework, interfacing with foot movement. At its best, biomechanics principles include measurement of spatial movement, calculating forces and studying the centre of gravity for different postural changes in the skeleton. Much of this is carried out in expensive gait laboratories, is grant-aided and forms the basis of research at the postgraduate (PG) level. This description illustrates some of the field of advanced MSK practice, although many independent practices install gait analysis equipment.

Podiatric sports medicine (PSM) cannot be studied to a high level as an undergraduate because there is insufficient room in the course for the breadth required. This subject is taught at PG level, often as a Diploma in Sports Medicine and at Master's level. Serious study allows podiatrists to go on to manage professional and amateur sportspeople. Again this subject will be covered later in more detail.

Students may observe podiatric surgery, which involves bones and joints of the foot. In addition, students will be able to undertake some skin surgery, including managing the infected ingrowing nail tissue, called onychocryptosis, after graduating. Local anaesthetic techniques are taught as a separate subject and skill within undergraduate courses. Usamah Khalid, Tim Kilmartin, Claire Freeman, Steve Kriss and Tony Wilkinson explain more about podiatric surgery in **Section 4**.

Placements versus On-Site Clinics

Creating exposure to the real world of podiatry for students has expanded over the last 50 years. All universities provide extended student exposure in the community and specialist clinics in hospitals.

Placements occur outside the university, while purpose-built facilities are used as simulation suites to help prepare the student to go out into clinical practice. Some universities still run in-house clinics with a reduced cost service to patient volunteers. Students can gain some idea of the contact experience under mentorship from their tutors.

Clinical exposure is continuous between years 1- 4 (4 in Scotland). The percentage of time in clinic increases year on year so final year students will spend more time with patient contact than in earlier years.

The following comments have been taken from lecturers and a few students from UK podiatry courses.

> Students will always prefer a placement because they get one to one supervision, which is something that is difficult for a university to provide. And so there's a huge tension there that often students will perennially complain that the placement is in some ways better, which of course it is if you're one to one with a practitioner. Supervisor manpower for placement-based models where it's all placement based can mean the NHS wouldn't be able to run the service, so we need to look at how we do placements more efficiently from that point of view. **Simon Otter** - *Lecturer Eastbourne, Brighton*

Innovation

The term placement is being expanded at Brighton. Third year students co-supervise first year students with staff.

> This means that the first years can have somebody with them much more than they ordinarily would. The third years can see how far they've come. The first years feel really comfortable with another student rather than a member of staff, and the third years put a huge amount of work in because they do not want to have knowledge exposed by a first-year student. **Simon Otter**

Third year students are encouraged to run peer-assisted study sessions. This will lead on to a particular topical area that first years find difficult and will run during lunchtime as seminars.

Student placements provide a rich experience because they will see a wider range of practices than if limited to one clinic. The training clinic style system is set out as a student might find in general practice.

> Our student placements have a number of different NHS Trusts and private practices that we use to allow students to access their clinical experiences. When we're asking students to determine what placements they want to go on throughout their three-year programme, we ask them to choose different placements so they don't spend their whole 1,000 hours in one NHS Trust, for example, provided that they're able to travel around to different places. **Phil Hendy**

Raymond Robinson, Head of School of Podiatry at Ulster, recognises that there are costs in running a clinic and this can make the course expensive to run given the numbers of staff required to supervise and train students with limited funding available from the Department of Health. Staff have built into the course an integrated placement model incorporating both NHS and private practice placements, which exposes students to multi-disciplinary healthcare practice and individual practice business models.

The Ulster Experience
> There is a minimal amount of placement in Year 1 beginning with an observational placement in the NHS and two weeks practical at the end of Semester 2. Placement is extended in Year 2 to about eight weeks in total over the year. The final year has a six-week NHS placement for students in semester two with some private practice placement. We have our own on-site patient clinic at the University for pre-placement training skills with heavily subsidised treatment costs for patients. **Raymond Robinson**

Using an acute hospital
> The main clinical placement for all students attending GCU is facilitated through a purpose-built outpatient Podiatry Department within the grounds of the Queen Elizabeth University Hospital, the largest acute hospital in Scotland. The Podiatry Department functions very much like a dental hospital and GP's, doctors, Podiatrists, and other health care practitioners can refer to this specialist department. Most of the treatment is provided by students. Clinical work starts in the first year where the student will manage

simple cases and the degree of patient complexity increased as the student progresses through the programme. By the end of the fourth year the undergraduate will have encountered many complex and challenging podiatric medical cases. Clinical education within an acute hospital allows students to attend placement within other clinical disciplines however relevant to Podiatry. One such placement was a consultant led vascular outpatient clinic, where the student would examine different images of the patient's arterial blood supply to the limb. The surgeon would explain the images, discuss the stenosis (blockage), ask the students questions relevant to the image and consider the potential surgical outcomes which were possible to revascularise the limb. Students were learning first hand from the consultant by examining the images and applying the relevant information from the patient to develop the management plan. The student placement at the Queen Elizabeth University Hospital enabled this learning experience. **Stuart Baird**

Stuart believes students are fortunate to have excellent links with Greater Glasgow and Clyde Health Board. The tie in with the Scottish Health Board, is equivalent to a Trust in England. This allows a wider exposure to clinical educators who are independent prescribers (I.P.) and where they have ultrasound and perform a variety of injections. Students are exposed to imaging in an acute hospital. A rounded experience within hospital clinical placements and in other parts of Scotland provide experience for different aspects of podiatric care.

Keen on surgery

I enjoyed scalpel debriding and working on psychomotor skills. I'm pleased I've done some kind of advanced sampling techniques like taking bone samples and soft tissue samples and things like that. We're taught in our university clinics, but my placement was in the diabetic limb service in Leeds. So you're dealing with people who are at risk of amputation. People with critical limb ischaemia, and so it's quite common for them to take bone samples of ulcers, probe into bone, and obviously that determines what kind of antibiotics are required. **Ethan Clifford**

Placement experience

Usually we would have been out on an eight-week block in our second semester of final year. But they allowed us to go two days a week from the start of the course, so every Thursday and Friday, I'm on placement in the hospital, here in Downpatrick. I've actually been able to go in once a month and carry out the nail surgeries, I think now, I've seventeen nail surgeries carried out by myself so far. **Paul Haughian**

Valuing foot health
I've just come up on placement and seeing high risk diabetic patients and MSK patients, and the difference comes from advising as well as treating. Patients say no one's put that much effort into me, or no-one's given me that extra five minutes to explain something to me. That's made such a difference. Encouraging that patient to value their own foot health and their own general health enough so that it comes to a matter of prevention rather than treatment. I think this is something I have valued during my last three years – managing skin conditions, infections and musculoskeletal problems. **Shuja Merban** - *student, Huddersfield*

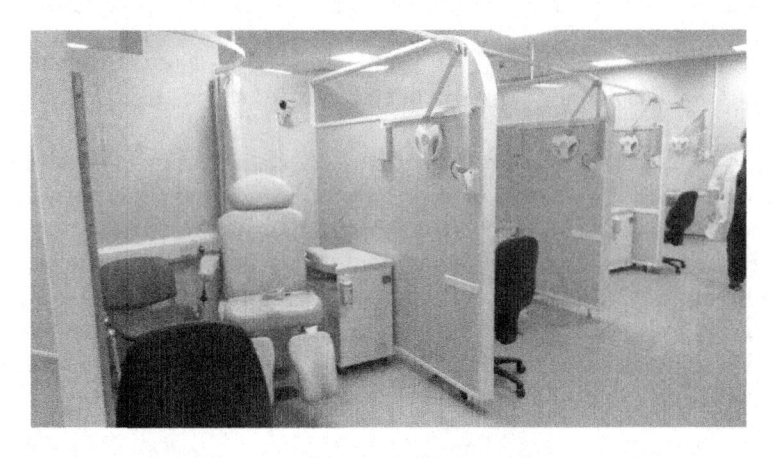

Picture author 2016 – University of Huddersfield – traditional style consulting booths

Clinical Units in Schools

Undegraduate Podiatry clinics in Schools have always had a modular layout. These provide space for instructors to circulate and maintain support for each student cohort. The units are different from NHS and private clinics (see p.27) where there is greater room. Teaching accommodation as show the provides a functionally effective space for each student with an environment of privacy. A curtain rail is shown to allow patients to change.

University is a place for debate, study, argument, challenge

The Bachelor Degree Curriculum

Each university course is different, but there are common themes between podiatry courses. While the curriculum below shows the blocks of subjects associated with podiatric medicine, courses also deal with a wide range of subjects by tutorials and examples of professional practice, often referred to as *softer skills* that have a deeper socio-philosophical basis. For students this stretches the mind and, in some ways, given modern healthcare settings are just as important.

Commencement of clinical studies

Courses start clinical studies at different times. The list below carries the main headings in an approximate year heading and should be taken only as a subject guide rather than a strict timetable. As Scotland has a four-year course structure, I have used the three-year model for Northern Ireland, Wales and England. Modules are taught to cover specific subjects (topics) and may be introductory or form whole study elements. Here are some examples of course subjects from different universities; health coaching conversations, business for podiatrists, research method and enquiry (*for the dissertation*). Influencing Innovation and Change, Pain: Theory and Management for Podiatrists. Very often modules (*lecture series to make a complete topic*) are split over several years gradually building on the complexity of that subject. The dissertation is completed in the final year.

Year One

Clinical skills & preparation for clinic – technique, sterilisation, basic wound care, dressings
Sciences wrap around medication, electrical and thermal treatments, human movement and measurement of forces. Biology involves cellular metabolism, tissue and organ function
Pathology includes wound healing and repair, immunity & infection
Anatomy may include cadaver human dissection
Physiology may be included in the first year
Mechanical therapy* manufacture and design of orthoses
Introduction to the library and how to access information and resources
First aid includes cardio-pulmonary resuscitation

*The term mechanical therapy may not be used universally. Originally coined by Northampton Nene College (podiatry) in 1985

Year Two

Anatomy advanced levels involves functional anatomy
Biomechanics studying human movement with computerised analysis
Pathology II cancer in the foot
Pharmacology has an emphasis on management of pain, inflammation and infection and local anaesthetic
Physiology - a good understanding of human biology is essential
Medicine (some move this to year 3 or split this between years)
Mechanical therapy II
Footwear and material science may blend in with other modules in the curriculum
Nail & skin surgery including theory and practice

Year Three

Medicine (includes haematology)
Surgery theory of podiatric and orthopaedic surgery with placements
Radiology also known as imaging X-rays, ultrasound, miscellaneous scans
Pathology theory
Pharmacology aligns independent prescribing theory alone
Practice management & Law (consent)
Mechanical therapy II
Advanced biomechanics

What people say about the Course

> In the first year, Cardiff focuses on foundational knowledge to include basic clinical skills – clinical hygiene and safety, infection control and how to approach patients. One of the most common benefits around podiatry is that it has a training programme that introduces students to patients early to give them confidence in dealing with people. **Ben Bullen** - *Lecturer, Cardiff*

In the second year, clinical skills are developed with greater involvement with musculoskeletal clinics. In the final year, involvement with podo paediatrics (*children's podiatry*) and high-risk clinics complement external placements

> We're quite fortunate, I suppose it being a relatively small population and we're obviously the only university that delivers a podiatry degree (in Wales). But I would say small, but perfectly well physically formed. The podiatry course has a partnership with Cardiff and Vale University Health Boards and we work with other health Boards throughout Wales to bring in specialist knowledge and skills. So practitioners with highly specialised skills and therefore quite a diverse caseload in house as well. **Ben Bullen**

As the number of clinics dedicated to patients has declined within the college-university environment, there is a greater reliance on the NHS, and its community placements. Cardiff provides two forms of clinic. Clinical delivery is subsidised within a private clinic and then a series of NHS clinics exist on site. The historical days set out a range of people exempt from payment for podiatry within the NHS. Free care was offered to those over 60, pregnant or nursing mothers up to two years. If you were under 16, or in full time undergraduate education the service was free. Those with learning difficulties and some disabilities were also eligible for free services. Diabetes and high risk were included with physician referrals.

> As the policies in the NHS have changed, many people seen historically for 'free' are no longer qualifying for NHS treatment, so they can be seen privately but by suitably skilled staff. The way people qualify for NHS now, is by being risk stratified, and of course largely we're talking about people with medical complexities. So diabetes being a classic category. Having diabetes alone would not qualify you on its own for NHS treatment, whereas before it might have. These days you need to then have at least an additional risk factor. So be that peripheral arterial disease or peripheral neuropathy.
> **Ben Bullen**

Similarities with the Plymouth course are notable with core medical conditions associated with the feet.

> Musculoskeletal conditions are taught through their second year as well to start developing their understanding of gait (*walking patterns and motion studies*) and the different pathologies that will come out of that side of things as well. In the third year, specific modules include minor surgery and pharmacology. **Phil Hendy**

Research is introduced earlier than some – in the second year. Problem-based scenarios form the method of solving problems rather than leaning on rote learning.

> Many NHS Trusts are using virtual assessments with their patients to make sure they're still keeping their numbers rolling through to see their patients in a safe environment. We're very keen to reintroduce our students into that world where virtual placements are carried out.
> **Phil Hendy**

Huddersfield University believes that working with a team you get on with is important as this provides a fruitful base to nurture creativity. The team bring variety, mentioning Dr Sarah Reel who takes a keen interest in forensic podiatry. Musculoskeletal work is forged by a team of three lecturers. Grace believed that it is important when teaching to remain with practice links. The nurture element is present, and staff encourage a relaxed approach to discussing elements of the course in a shared space where formality is replaced with soft furniture and cups of tea.

Huddersfield runs clinics as modular teams which are linked to the theory (*didactics*) for that year group.

> The objective is to help provide a link from theory to practice so the student can really visualise why they need to know what's been delivered in the theory lectures. So for me, it is crucial to their learning. We don't just stand at the front of the class, talking at them for four hours, you know. Let's say it's looking at the knee, we might talk for 20 minutes then demonstrate knee assessments, discuss how this links to the foot and the whole framework. **Grace Parfit** – *Lecturer, University of Huddersfield*

Modern podiatry education encapsulate training and studying in areas that are not focused on the foot alone.

Modular teaching

The modular method of teaching crosses most techniques and pushes students to enquire, challenge, read and research so they can become aware of medical and physiological aspects of human foot movement, thus applying their knowledge of anatomy. Within this framework the person is not a number or a condition, but has to be assessed specifically for mental and social implications. The realisation that medicine has changed and should be tailor-made has become ever more important. Teachers have the challenge in keeping up with new techniques to deliver information so the podiatrist is able to leave university equipped for most eventualities, but can adapt on their own because they have the tools to make adjustments outside the official texts.

Clinical structure in Scotland's Glasgow Caledonian University

Looking at the structure of the programme at Glasgow's Caledonian

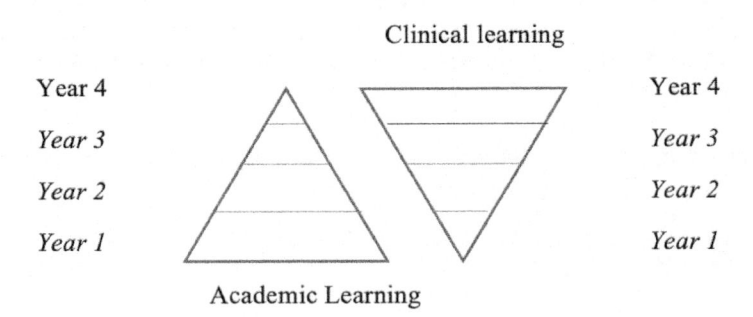

```
                    Clinical learning
Year 4                   △  ▽                Year 4
Year 3                  /  \/  \              Year 3
Year 2                 /   /\   \             Year 2
Year 1                /___/  \___\            Year 1
                    Academic Learning
```

University, first year students might be in clinic or a simulation lab and then in the clinic at the Queen Elizabeth Hospital. First year was a half day a week. The second year, it was one day, a week, the third year was one a half days a week, and the fourth year was a full two days per week.

In Scotland the undergraduate degree in Podiatry is of four years duration and clinical exposure starts almost immediately in the first year. Initially, the new student will be exposed to simulated patient care within the simulation lab at the University, however will rapidly progress to uncomplicated patient care at the Department of Podiatry located within the grounds of the Queen Elizabeth University Hospital in Glasgow. During the first year the student will spend 0.5 days per week in clinic, in second year this increases to one full day per week. The third year again increases to 1.5 days per week and finally in the fourth year the student will spend two full days per week developing their management techniques of complex podiatric medical pathology.

The theoretical academic component is a mirror image of the clinical exposure albeit in reverse. In the first year the student will spend most of their time in the university attending lectures and tutorials providing a broad base of academic learning while in the fourth year most academic work centres around the student dissertation and a couple of other modules such as Contemporary Podiatric Practice and into Employment.

A Career in Podiatric Medicine

> At GCU the degree tries to balance both clinical and academic learning. This can be compared to two pyramids - one of which is inverted. In the first year if you think of a pyramid, the bottom provides the broad base of academic learning while the inverted pyramid provides the small clinical component. This proportion of learning is reversed when the student progresses to the fourth year when the student maximises patient care. **Stuart Baird**

The academic work is the other way around. From the first year the broad base of academic work tapers off through the years into the fourth year when during the last semester, students would engage in their dissertation and a couple of other modules. Most courses introduce clinical work in the first year and this grows exponentially as the student progresses into the final year, be it Scotland, England, Wales or Northern Ireland. Students and graduates often use the affectionate term *'Pods'* for their profession.

One student's journey

> In the first year the student studies a broad foundation in anatomy. General and regional anatomy form the basis of the module and in particular the structure and biomechanical function of the limb are considered in depth. Physiology is another major component studied in the first year where the normal structure and function of the body systems are studied, ie cell function through to the cardiovascular system. The student will also study Podiatric Pathology and an Introduction to Podiatric Practice

> In the second year, the student starts to develop their clinical skills in more detail, while at the same time developing an understanding of disease and medicine. The student at this point will study modules in Pathophysiology, Medicine, Musculo skeletal structure function and disease and research methodology. Additionally, the student is introduced to surgery including podiatric surgery and the basic principles of orthopaedic management

> In the third year, the student begins to develop the more specialised areas of podiatric practice and will study in detail "The High-Risk Foot" including vascular disease and diabetes. At this point in the programme treatment of musculoskeletal disease is further developed along with the introduction of imaging techniques such as medical ultrasound to assist with diagnosis. Appropriate rehabilitation for this group of patients is also introduced at this point. In the third year the student is introduced to local anaesthesia, prescription only medicines and the principals of podiatric surgery. It should be remembered that at the point of graduation and

registration with the Health and Care Professions Council all students will be able to administer local anaesthesia and provide on a sale and supply basis of a number of prescription only medicines including basic antibiotic therapy.

In the fourth year, the student further develops the area of clinical practice and will start to consolidate learning particularly around the management of the complex patient. Additionally, the student prepares to enter practice and completes a module entitled "Into Employment". A large component of the fourth year is the completion of the student's dissertation. **Nancy Keller** *(4th year student)* **with Stuart Baird**

Scotland's Queen Margaret's University (QMU)

Although Stephanie was from an older Alumni, she attended when a fourth year was offered. The fourth year is not the threshold period of study.

> Quite a lot of people just wanted to go out and start working and earning money after three years. I don't think I would have been ready to go out into the profession without that fourth year which provided a valuable industrial year. **Stephanie Owen** - *former student, Edinburgh*

Masters in Science (MSc) courses have started to develop at different universities throughout the UK. QMU has developed different entry-level qualifications and provides graduates with several options for a fulfilling career in podiatry. All podiatry courses help people improve their health, well-being, and quality of life.

One is called a **Master of Podiatry (MPod).** The MPod is an undergraduate Masters course which provides an option to transfer to the BSc route at the end of Year Two. The other course is an **MSc Podiatry (Pre-Registration) course** delivered full-time, over two years with a clinical and health promotion focus. All courses lead to the eligibility to apply for registration with the HCPC as a podiatrist. Within the last few years, a collaborative partnership with The SMAE Institute Ltd. offers a 4-year BSc (Hons) Podiatry, with a HE Dip Assistant Practitioner (Podiatry) exit after completion of 2 years. The award is offered by QMU, and the programme is delivered by the SMAE Institute through a blended elearning route. Completion leads to eligibility to apply for HCPC registration. *See section 6 closing notes for more information.*

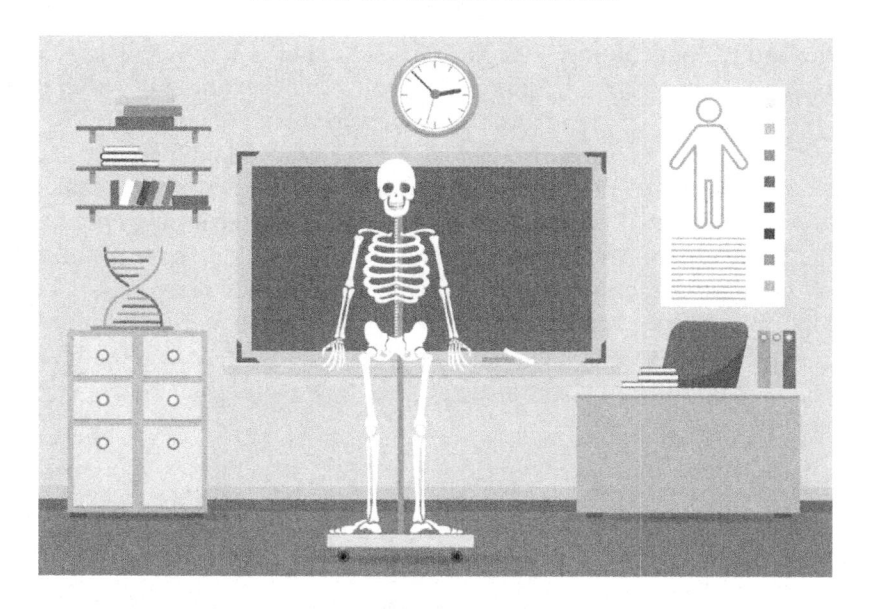

Anatomical dissection

No matter which aspect of podiatry you wish to practice you will need anatomy. You might find the next section a bit gruesome but we are health professionals, scientists and researchers and this is our role. The podiatrist must learn every single muscle in the lower limb and know which nerve and blood vessel supplies both muscle and joint. Not all courses use cadaver classes so discuss any fears you may have before you get to the anatomy dissection class. Cadavers are difficult to come by legally and there is strict regulation over human tissue. The trend set by Burke and Hare; the infamous grave robbers of Edinburgh no longer exists – but once upon a time cadavers were delivered to anatomists by order!

Prosected specimens are common where a cadaver has been dissected to show the structures without students being involved. Today anatomy is taught with 3D computerised models making access easier, but moving away from the pretty colours, anatomy looks different in the flesh!

> We have moved completely away from dissection to 3D anatomy tables (we are using Anatomage www.anatomage.com). This allows us to integrate pathology and imaging in a way we never have before. The enhanced digital engagement is popular with students. **Simon Otter**

If you are lucky or unlucky enough to encounter a cadaver please don't worry about ethics. All parts are buried with attention to dignity after their use. I should add – leaving your body to science is the term used for this type of work unless organ transplants can be used. Many patients cannot provide their organs due to age, disease or infection. If you do enter an anatomy laboratory prepare to be confronted by the sweet sickly pungency of the smell of the dissection laboratory; the pallor of the legs and feet. Keen on fictional crime I noted that Nick Dixon's pathologist in his Damien Boyd series recommends placing 'Vick's Vapour Rub' under the nose to offset the smells. I cannot comment as I had to suck it up, but that smell is something you never forget. Ektaa, however, found the experience revealing -

Experience at the Leicester Medical School laboratory.
> If you've never done dissections before, there is no prepping you for that. It was jarring for a lot of students as well. So it took a minute to adjust to that. When you think about the information that you're learning, you adjust very quickly. The lecturers do mention that dissections are part of this course, so I was prepared but not as prepared as when you're actually walking into a dissection room and you're dissecting a leg, for example. So that was quite an exciting experience. **Ektaa Vadgama** - *student, Northampton*

Why do we dissect?

The role of a university is to provide a seat of learning for students by employing skilled educationalists. The educationalist is trained first in podiatry and then will have added a teaching qualification. Being experienced in their field, they know that modern podiatry is a science subject based around medicine and so it is imperative to adopt a close model to medicine so each student leaves university with a rounded knowledge, acquired skills and a healthy enquiring mind. We never know when we need to acquire further information and develop skills. We will have a broad knowledge of medicine that we might never use, but if we want to take up independent prescribing (see later), we will find the tools taught on the course essential for our further development. In much the same way, an introduction to cadaveric dissection can prepare us for advanced work in MSK, electromyographic studies as well as surgical knowledge.

If you have attended an undergraduate dissection module you will repeat this all over again when studying for foot surgery. Research often commences with human tissue, and cadaver studies litter the annals of research studies.

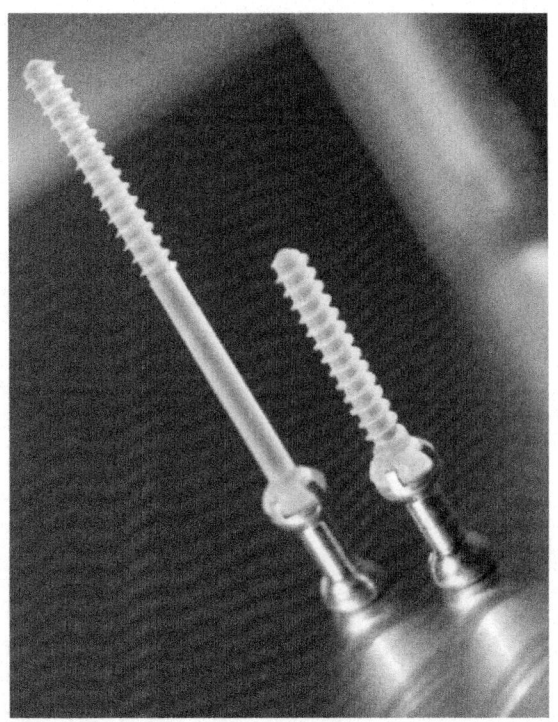

https://musculoskeletalkey.com/absorbable-biomaterials/ c/o A.S Landsman Accessed 28/9/22

Research screw fixation for bone
My NHS Trust were engaged in a project to study the value of screws which would absorb (see image) after a period of time when bone would have healed. To test the method before attempting to use the screws on living patients, we used a cadaver at one of the medical schools – a rather elderly man of 70 who had donated his body to science. **David Tollafield**

All studies require a system for testing students' ability. Good communication is part of routine practice. Podiatrist Nick Knight demonstrates foot anatomy to one of his patients using a model foot. c/o NK Active

Examination and Assessment

O.S.C.Es (Objective Structured Clinical Examination) are currently used to ensure students attain skills in areas essential to their field. Inevitably educationalists believe this method allows better assessment and ties to key elements of theory within a course, e.g taking blood pressure, undertaking a urine test, using a doppler system to listen to blood flow, perform first aid and cardio-pulmonary resuscitation, identify capillary filling time or use an oximeter to measure oxygen flow in the lower limb, measure an ankle-brachial index. The student must explain the findings to the assessor-tutor. Educational methods constantly change to balance the most accurate method so OSCE's may not be used by all universities or may be mixed with other methods.

The feared viva voce or oral examination still exists in some cases but is less dramatic than in the days of the older courses. Continuous assessment and assignments form a good portion of course work assessment alongside the practical skills and OSCEs. Written examination papers cannot be avoided as these illustrate recall, accurate thought processes and written communication skills.

The Dissertation & Thesis

Most courses will introduce the subject of research and statistics in the latter part of the second year. The dissertation is part of the final year. Students need to consider their chosen subject early on. The dissertation together with continuous course assessment grades make up the honours section of the BSc degree i.e BSc (Hons) graded at 2.2, 2.1 and 1 (first class honours).

All students must understand how to read a scientific paper, many are crammed with statistical tests, much of which can be irrelevant. There are good papers and poor papers and the student should know how to disassemble a paper and read its value. The idea of reading papers is borne early in the course and will appear in the first year. Students may be taught how to work on a theme together or choose their own theme. The level is basic and often allows students to consider the academic side of podiatry. You will be able to read many stories from podiatrists who have entered the clinical field to build on podiatric medical science. Dr Simon Otter points out -

> The dissertation is very quantitative focused, if papers don't have relevant statistics they don't get published. There is real value in both qualitative approaches and service delivery/clinical governance projects. **Simon Otter**

Marking

The dissertation is marked separately from the course but contributes towards the degree grade. Computers today check for 'copying' known as plagiarism for many formal assignments and dissertations. In educational circles plagiarism is a form of academic misconduct. There is no doubt about it that plagiarism is making fraud against those persons who are original authors. You cannot copy and insert work from other sources into your assignment! The student must interpret and analyse work, referencing any citations correctly to attribute passages to the original authors.

Research is an exciting topic
> I think the profession needs to progress to PhD level and research the things that we know help, where they are not backed up necessarily with enough good evidence. **Emily Reaney**

The options for research are growing and there are help grants available for those with an academic interest. The undergraduate research programmes however have to be tailored to fit time, access to material, viable ethics approval and educational objectivity.

> Our team developed a survey and to review the efficacy of the lateral (insole) wedges in managing osteoarthritis. **Ethan Clifford**

Ethan Clifford's research project included a 2000-3000 word assignment, one for high-risk podiatry, and the other was a project conducted within a research team. He admits Covid changed some of their aspirations and a literature review was substituted, but he tried to do it in an area that he was interested in. A literature review is a piece of work looking at a wide range of material from published research with the ability to critically comment and evaluate its contribution to the subject by academic argument. Literature reviews are the primary anchor upon which research is built.

Catriona Doyle studied at Northampton University where she was in her final year working on ankle brachial pressure index (ABPI) as part of a diagnosis of peripheral arterial disease. Ryan approached his study from the basis of musculoskeletal studies around physiology. This area of human movement would come under podiatric sports medicine. It seemed logical to take in this study given his passion for cycling. He wanted to look at and alter riders' saddle positions to see how that affects power output and muscle fatigue by measuring resistance and controlling the distance.

A Career in Podiatric Medicine

I would drop it down two inches, and we do a minute effort on each saddle height. The results suggest that the two-inch lower drop improves power and distance travelled. Keen cyclists and the people just getting into it, would probably benefit from these alterations. Research papers suggested the knee angles and stuff like that. So it's measuring the angles. In comparison to obvious knee injuries, that's the only one I found was quite similar. So there's knee injuries and muscle fatigue using actual knee angle. **Ryan Brain**

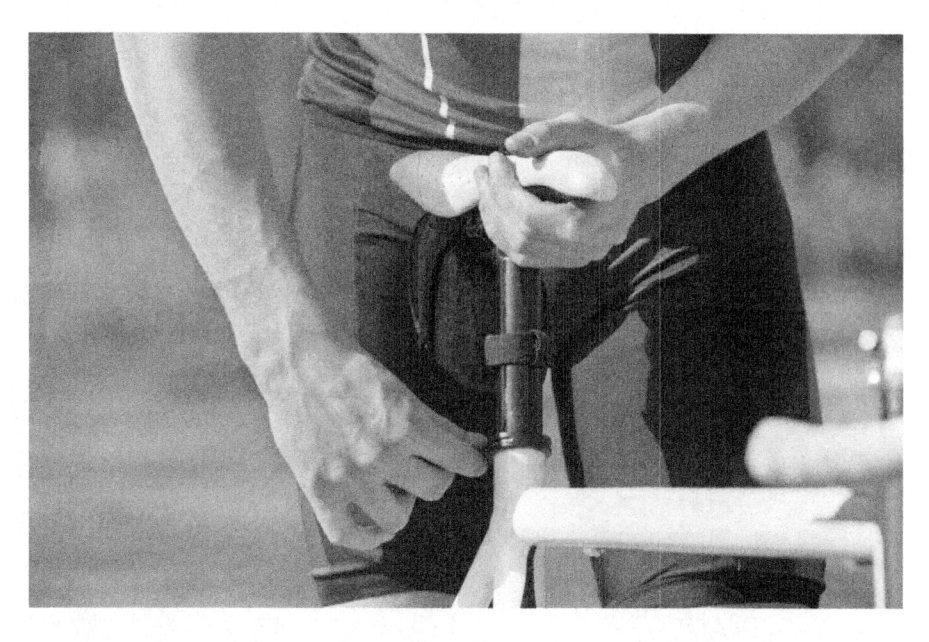

Students are encouraged to pick topics of interest to them but also to show how to use research methodology

Tollafield

Public speaking is both an art and a skill required to overcome nerves, provide clarity of thought and offer creativity. Students today are taught to be able to present topics at conference which assists these skills and contributes toward their educational portfolio (see list by author at the end of this book 'Projecting Your Image').

Learning to Speak in Public

Speaking, writing and body language make effective communication better. Podiatry is a patient contact profession and succeeds where communication skills are optimised. Students are made aware of expanding their communication skills with patients, but also when speaking to other professionals.

Promoting podiatry and your own contribution is essential, and with new tools such as video (YouTube) and podcasts, modern communication relies on voice, presentation and capturing the audience. Of course, this does not come naturally to most and so it has to be acquired.

The first year was exciting
> We had to do presentations on functional anatomy. I didn't realise that I would be so nervous presenting. The entire time I was shaking. Luckily, I had practised in front of a mirror for weeks, so I knew what I had to say at what slide. So I didn't have to constantly look at my slide or look at my piece of paper. So it was good, but oh, boy, the nerves! **Ektaa Vadgama**

All podiatrists who train for a career toward podiatric surgery are expected as part of their postgraduate programme to present at conference. This skill should not be confined to one area of our work. In other cases, presentations are now expected at interview, making a bid for research or seeking a committee's help to improve your budget.

Even if we do not used the skill formally, practitioners will find talking to local groups easier about their service to promote both their skill and deliver health education.

Positive feedback
> Although I am a seasoned public speaker, having taught for over 30 years including being a university lecturer – my first experience as a graduate was a disaster. There is nothing like being prepared. The disaster fortunately made me determined to do better next time. I was confronted by someone who had attended my lamentable first effort on a second occasion.
>
> *"That was so much better David, your last talk was crap!"* **David Tollafield** (taken from *Presenting Your Image. From Conferences to Village Halls*)

Which direction to go after qualifying?

A BSc (Hons) in Podiatry provides a basis for learning and allows you to treat a variety of low-risk conditions until the induction period has been completed within some NHS Trusts. A year is considered appropriate by some, a few years by others.

> It depends on each Trust and the training. University of Southampton graduates normally consolidate their learning within six months and if they take on the responsibility and meet the competencies they quickly progress. Most students who join the NHS will see moderate and higher risk patients because this is the case load, they are commissioned to treat. **Benjamin Jones**

After graduation

By the time the third or fourth year graduate emerges they will have a broad knowledge of the foot and the science behind function and disease. They will be eligible to start in private practice or enter the NHS – usually as an AfC (*Agenda for Change*) Band 5. While mature students will be more confident in going directly into practice if they have former skills, school entrants benefit from mentorship and shadowing, often from within the NHS. (*See Victoria North*)

The first year is usually spent gaining experience under a senior podiatrist, someone who is willing to provide mentorship. Many students have to be reminded that they have a wealth of up-to-date knowledge but their experience is limited to their exposure at school-college.

The loss of graduates is a concern to any profession, be it medicine or other medically-based professions. Much has to do with understanding what is available, what is normal and what a graduate can or cannot do. Let's discuss this concept further. Similar to your driving test, you acquire the essential skills, but it takes a few years to become a good driver despite being competent. Road conditions dictate your learning and you will have to allow for meeting other drivers who approach you. Refinement is part of learning and creates any type of skill.

The NHS provides mentorship for those at AfC 5 (*see Sarah Twiss*) as some supervision is still considered important. If you wish to study and expand toward the high-risk foot, the NHS is the best place. If you wish to study towards MSK podiatry, then the choices are wider, but the independent sector has more flexibility. Podiatric surgery is contained within the NHS because of access to funding and placement exposure.

> One of our attractions is the Master's programme. Of course, some won't want to undertake postgraduate courses initially, but depending upon where a graduate sees his or herself, postgraduate skills can open up both the private and NHS sectors. **Grace Parfitt**

Advanced techniques

Graduates will always have to invest in further practical study to improve practice and employment opportunities, and this should be made clear at the outset for most health professions. The question that will always remain is *"who pays?"*

Podiatry is an evolving profession which means what is not mainstream today will become normal practice tomorrow. Many technical treatments, such as low power laser and extra corporeal shock wave therapy, are now available to undergraduates while ultrasound diagnostics is catching up. Those wanting to expand quickly will find there is plenty to stimulate clinical progress.

Where possible I have tried to give reasons why bolt-on courses are required and not mainstreamed within the BSc curriculum. You can leave university and practice without having further skills, except for must-do courses – known as basic life support. It is up to each person to decide if they want to sub-specialise, become expert in one field and make this a career such as high-risk or foot surgery.

Most universities offer programmes to allow graduates to develop further but each may develop different subjects of interest. The majority of graduates are keen to be competitive and this is where the bolt-on system plays an invaluable part. Universities offer advanced courses as higher degrees and diplomas. The Royal College of Podiatry and Institute of Chiropodists & Podiatrists have a wide range of schemes which they accredit, giving you assurance that this is an agreed course to take to extend your clinical skills.

In the NHS, there is a natural desire to progress and, where support is available, retention of NHS podiatrists is assured.

> I would love to progress further up in podiatry, definitely. I do need to narrow my focus. I've given myself two years actually. I want to be in an AfC Band 7 in a lead role. I'm torn at the moment between vascular and nail surgery. Nail surgery is quite niche, and I think if I go there I will just pigeonhole myself a little bit more. So maybe high-risk nail surgery with a hint of vascular might be where I go with this kind of thing. But I want to do more research. I would like to go for a Master's definitely, and I would like to get more of a lead role. I would like to sing podiatry from the rooftops and promote it

alot more. Getting higher up as well gives you the ability to do more, which is what I want to do. **Sarah Twiss**

Advanced techniques should be considered in the context of clinical skills developed at the end of a podiatry course. Many podiatrists go on to advance their skills in life-support.

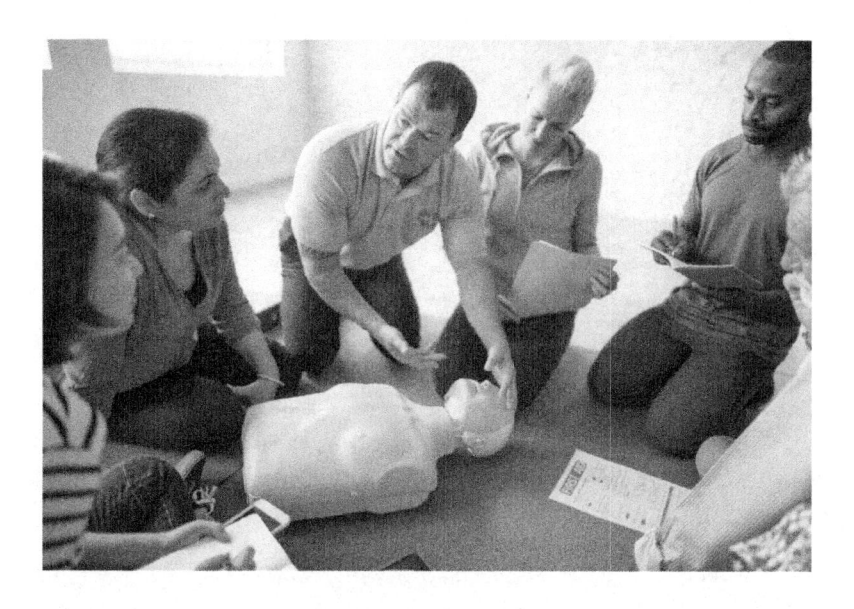

Life support (rescusitation) is part of the duty of all health care professionals and starts with basic life-support moving later to advanced techniques

Local anaesthesia

All universities provide a course in nail surgery and introduce local anaesthesia during the course while other medical injections are limited.

> Beyond local anaesthetics, other prescription only medicines is not something that we would introduce at undergraduate level at the moment. I think that is something that we do as qualified clinicians as postgraduate study and under appropriate clinical supervision. I think at undergraduate level we would probably struggle with finding appropriate patients to give the students enough clinical experience. **Phil Hendy**

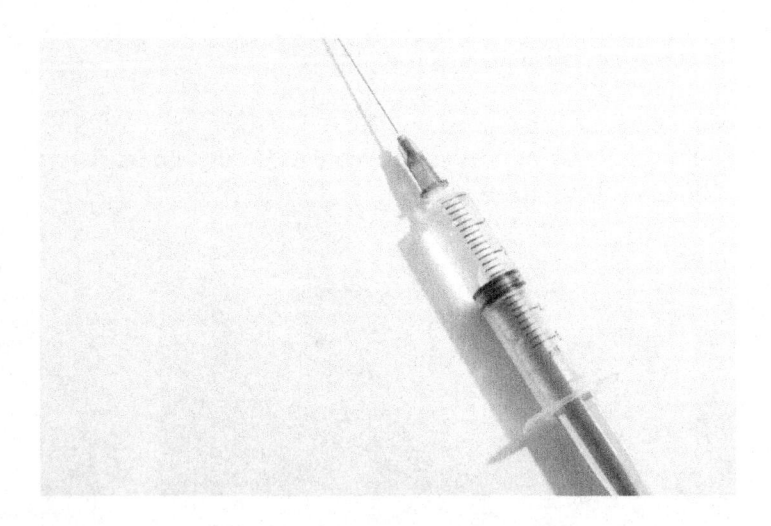

Podiatrists developed local anaesthetic-based treatment during the 1970s which led to surgery

Local anaesthetic (LA) is important for performing some treatment activities painlessly. LA can also be used to differentiate painful areas in order to aid diagnosis, which extends its value in clinical practice.

Many students who enter podiatry want to undertake surgery, which is a long process where clinical placements are extended at postgraduate level by many years. Anaesthesia has advanced considerably with blockades being provided at knee level as well as within the foot.

Basic skin surgery techniques are also practiced without the need to undertake the surgical fellowship. Both the Royal College of Podiatry and the Institute of Chiropodists & Podiatrists offer advanced skin surgery courses.

A Career in Podiatric Medicine

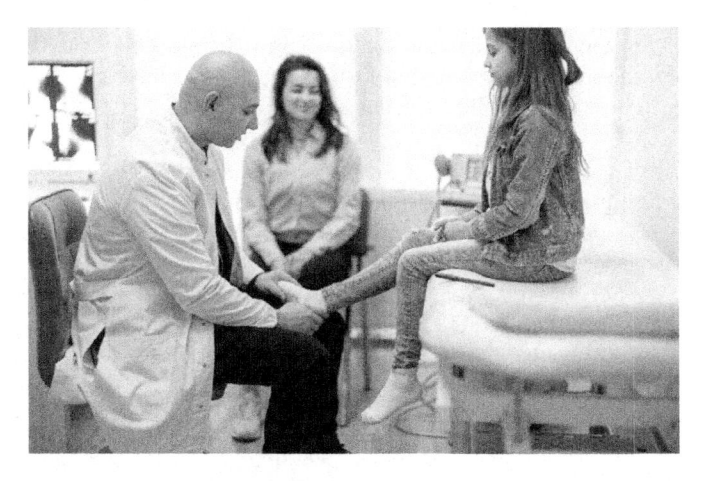

Children's Podiatry

Paediatric podiatry is not so well developed in the undergraduate course curriculum, but has gained ground over the years.

> Children make up approximately ten percent of podiatry's caseload. It is relatively common for children to experience podiatry related conditions, one in four children experience musculoskeletal pain, one in a thousand children have arthritis, over five percent are born with a foot problem, over ten percent of children have conditions affecting movement, five percent of children walk on their toes and foot pain is the most common of all musculoskeletal problems in the teenage population. *(Royal College of Podiatry – Guide to Paediatrics in Podiatry)*

Ben Bullen came from an Australian training background. Australia has a diversified profession, strongly steeped in sports medicine. Ben has tried to developed paediatric care in the UK. One of the common mistakes many make is they call podiatry 'paediatric' as the sound is similar to some ears. The term Podo-paediatrics was developed in the USA around the many centres which added child foot health to the US curriculum. James Ganley, Ron Valmassy and Harold Schoenhuass are but a few of the epic names associated with children's foot health.

> The best way to manage the paediatric patient is in a team environment. Within our field I think perhaps you've got different pathways and different health Boards. I'm thinking about some places that might prefer to refer everything to physios, for example, but things are changing, aren't they? We're looking at one of the front runners up in Scotland, in Greater Glasgow and Clyde, where all foot

and ankle problems are being triaged through podiatry, and that Glasgow model is being adopted further and further throughout the four nations of the UK. **Ben Bullen**

There are currently paediatric modules within the MSc programmes at Brighton and Stafford. There used to be a stand-alone PGDip at Glasgow in podo-paediatrics. There are very few podiatrists who work exclusively in paediatrics. Most members for the Children's Podiatry Special Advisory Group have their paediatric caseload bunched in with their MSK clinic. **James Welch**

James Welch, is involved with the Royal College of Podiatry framework incorporating learning and developmental milestones for podiatrists to become skilled in the area of paediatric podiatry.

The NHS does focus on children's foot health problems and always has. Once you could see a plethora of verruca (wart) clinics but policies change and this was whittled down, much finding its way to the independent sector. Talking to Sarah she uses the common term 'Paeds' for paediatrics.

> We have clinicians that do paediatric biomechanics. They have babies coming in, one-year olds with flat feet. Sometimes it's all about managing expectations with the parents. Our MSK podiatrist, Pete, he's just amazing. He's great with the children. We've got a trial going at the moment, which Pete's heading up, which is young people - between age 8 and 14 with flatfoot deformity and looking at stretches, orthoses and combinations of both. So anyone we see at the moment in community that fits those criteria are entered into the *'Ostrich Trial.'* **Sarah Twiss**

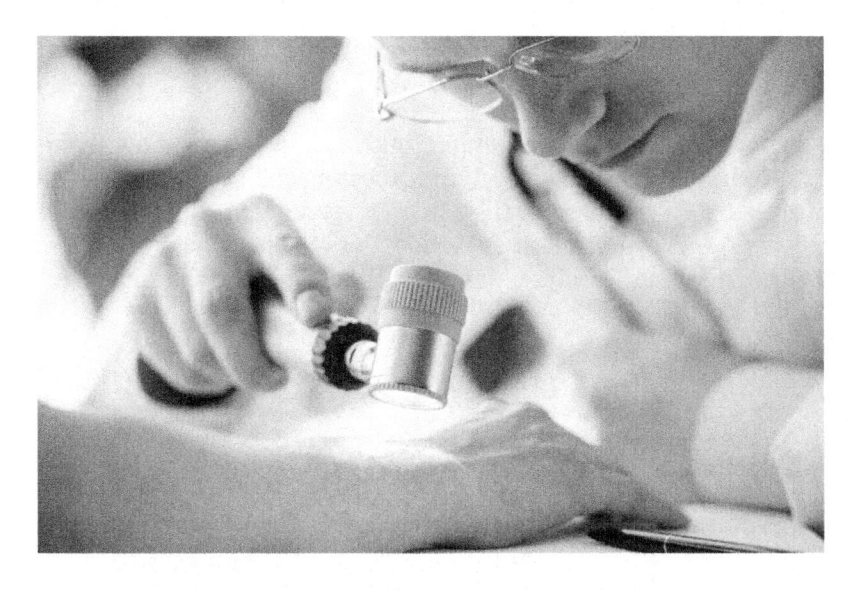

The dermatoscope is now an important tool for assessing skin, whether this is on hands or feet

Dermatology

Dermatology does not have a pathway compared to other areas of podiatry. Cardiff University offers a Diploma in dermatology and the University of Hertfordshire provides a MSc in dermatology skills and is open to all healthcare professionals from all over the world. It can be done part-time or full-time. The course marries wound care, offering a good crossover with a lot of entrants because wound care and dermatology are quite closely related.

Podiatrists are now pushing at the boundaries using a device called a dermatoscope. The technique has primarily been in the hands of dermatologists, but this has made its way into primary care and we're now seeing GPs use this technique. Dermatology sits well with podiatrists. Specialist tools are not required, and the practice fits into the independent sector.

> With more podiatrists involved, we are detecting cancers earlier and literally saving lives. There is plenty of work out there for anybody who's interested to wander into that specialism. We don't have enough dermatologists. This is why dermatology specialist nurses

have grown. Nurses are now doing things that the dermatologist used to do. **Ivan Bristow**

It is difficult to predict the future, but with medicine now seen as something of a tangle and training not meeting the needs of the nation, podiatry can infill with specialist areas to safeguard the provision for healthcare. A new generation of school leavers now have the distinct advantages of seeing a profession where, like Ivan, they can find a niche.

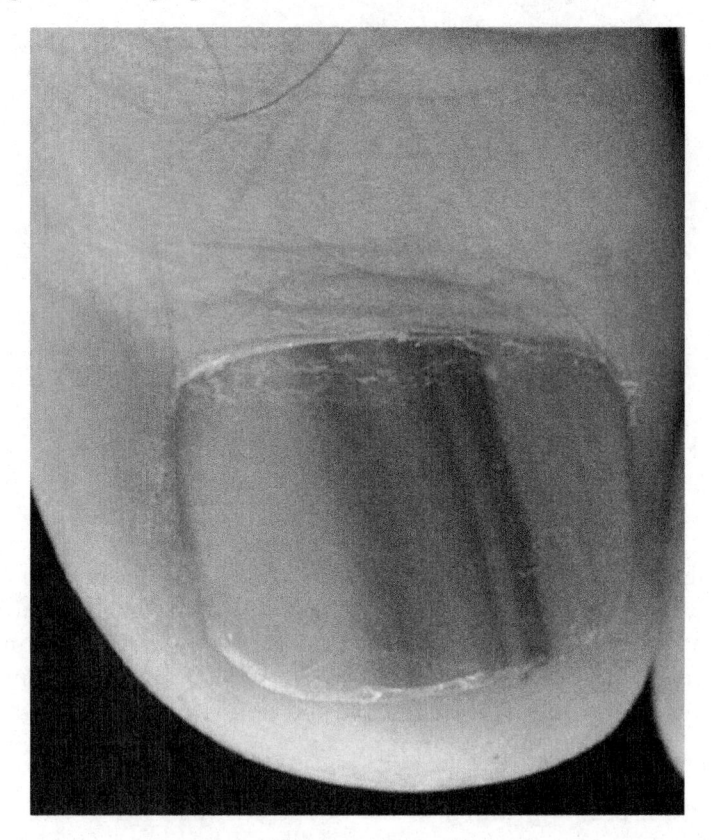

© Dr P H Abimelec c/o Dermnetnz.org
Melanoma of the nail bed can present in different ways and is now part of a large project within podiatry to provide patients with better screening from this condition, which if left untreated leads to early death.

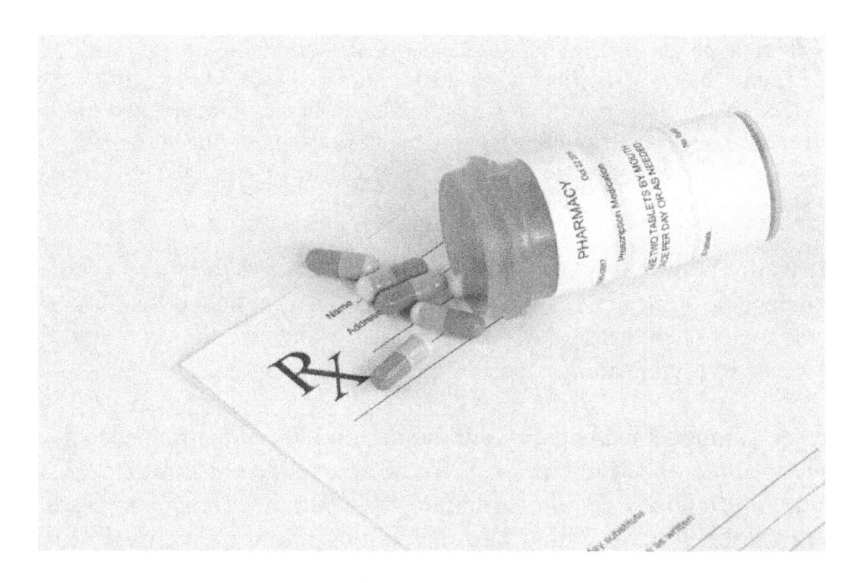

Independent prescribing (I.P.)

Universities do not have sufficient qualified staff prescribing or active patient cases that can be monitored safely to meet the standards that an I.P. course requires. Where those podiatrists have gained an I.P. qualification, noted on the HCPC register, they have had a mentor throughout the process. I.P started with nurses and has slowly expanded with podiatrists being among one of the top user groups.

> You start the basic process at undergraduate level to equip students with the tools so they're familiar with the drug names and the pharmacological effects. So it makes it easy for them to slide into I.P.
> **Andy Bridgen** - *Lecturer University of Huddersfield*

Injectable Steroids

It takes time for one end of a profession to catch up where skills and scope do not match. Podiatric surgeons and Extended Scope Podiatrists (ESPs) use steroids extensively in their practice, but general podiatrists have only in recent years added these skills. Steroid injections have become one of the fastest bolt-on skills.

> We did a top-up, two-day programme, for continuous professional development (CPD). While our podiatry students graduate with

pharmacology and injection skills (local anaesthetic) they aren't taught injection skills with locations for steroid injections. Competency for injection skills tends to be underdeveloped in practice because there are very few mentors to support development of this and so progression is much slower than we expected. **Cathy Bowen** - *Lecturer University of Southampton*

While Cathy admits this is disappointing and has yet to be resolved, she acknowledges there are really good centres of excellence that focus on musculoskeletal injuries and rehabilitation. The problem is that they cannot take everyone and so they're few and far between.

At present, students who qualify will have a number of medicines that they can access under the Medicines Act. To be able to inject steroid drugs such as methyl prednisolone, the graduate will require some postgraduate support. At the time of writing, this element of practice remains confusing largely due to the lack of access to mentorship. However, in time this omission to the undergraduate course will change. Podiatrists have always been able to access medications and sell or provide these to patients. The group of medicines - often called 'drugs' – are regulated and so while many can be bought over the counter, antibiotics and anaesthetic are listed as prescription only medicines (POMs). Podiatrists are one group of AHPs who can take a course in I.P. This is not taught on the university course at present, but as a bolt-on course for many this is the way forward.

> Steroid injections could easily become part of the undergraduate programme, but Independent Prescribing is probably too big a step. Students might have the textbook knowledge about prescribing but the softer professional skills that are gained through experience would be missing. Newly qualified students are pretty unsure about how to use prescription only medicines (POMs) which form a relatively short list. I think there is scope for them to understand pharmacology better, because obviously we very much focus on the POMs and medication and their interactions. **Andy Bridgen**

> It's essential nowadays as podiatry is taking a medical direction. My last role with the NHS was very medical in terms of making the decisions about patient care. A lot of that was sometimes an appreciation of the pharmacology. Independent prescribing is the way forward for our profession. It's having the confidence to have those conversations with doctors and have to being able to have the same level pegging dialogue even with the orthopaedic surgeon.
> **Keri Hutchinson** - *Lecturer, Cardiff Metropolitan University*

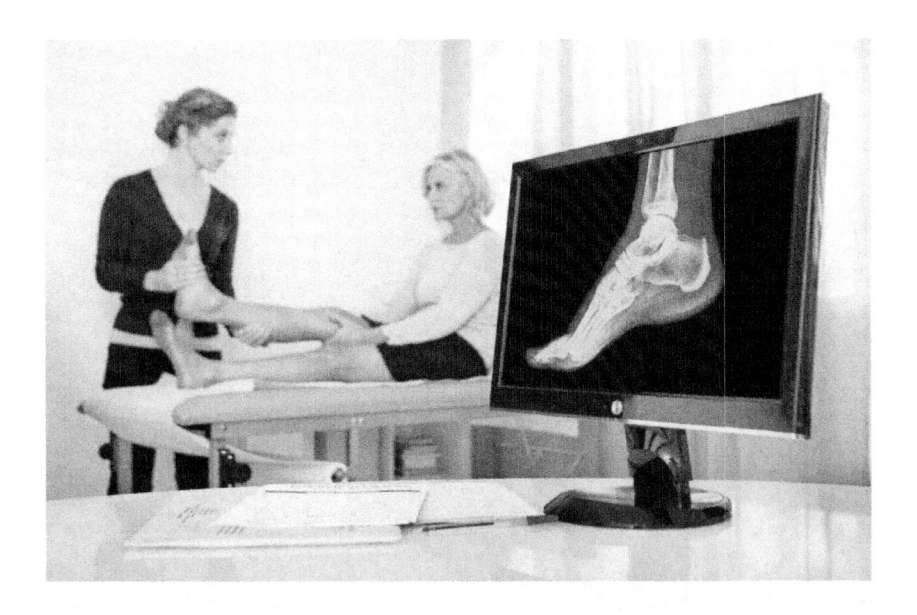

Imaging using radiological techniques to identify pathology

Imaging

The best-known imaging method is X-ray. It is safe and relatively cheap. All courses will give a grounding in imaging so that you will understand what imaging is available. Ultrasound (US) does not use radiation and has no risk from this source. It is easy to access as equipment is small. Podiatrists are now including US in their clinics to help place injections. Advanced imaging includes scanners; computerised tomography, scintigraphy and magnetic resonance scanners. Each have their place in podiatric orthopaedics, MSK, high-risk and surgery, but they are not accessible without further training.

To undertake ordinary X-rays, access to a hospital or radiology facility is required in the UK which requires a radiology protection course (IRMER). Access in the NHS may be easier as the clinician works within a standard framework, while in independent practice, podiatrists must make arrangements with the NHS or independent facilities to gain official and legal access.

Some MSc courses in podiatry provide interpretation of imaging, but there are courses designed for health professionals in ultrasound.

Gap year options

While you have heard about gap years before going to university, there are options to take time out to develop new skills before working full-time.

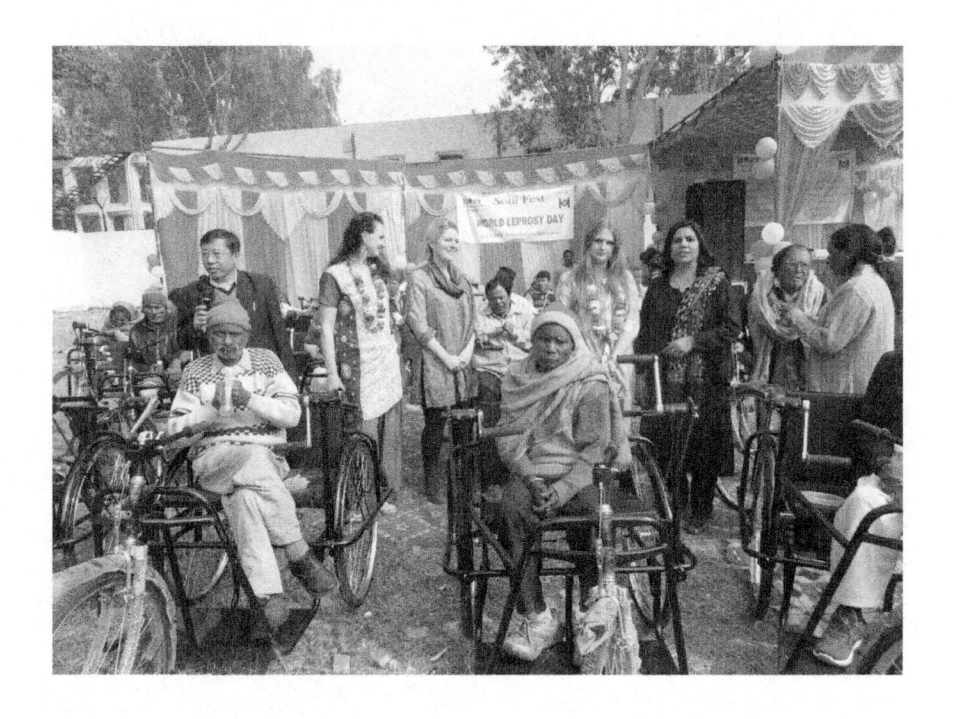

A scene from her overseas experience at a Leprosy centre. Courtesy of Alison Clarke-Morris

A Career in Podiatric Medicine

WE WANT YOU Podiatrist

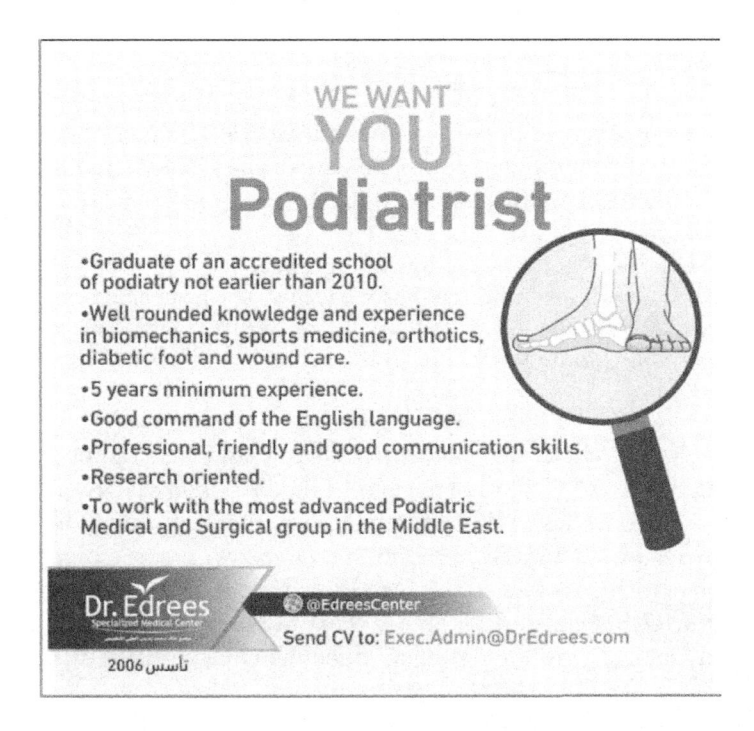

- Graduate of an accredited school of podiatry not earlier than 2010.
- Well rounded knowledge and experience in biomechanics, sports medicine, orthotics, diabetic foot and wound care.
- 5 years minimum experience.
- Good command of the English language.
- Professional, friendly and good communication skills.
- Research oriented.
- To work with the most advanced Podiatric Medical and Surgical group in the Middle East.

Dr. Edrees Specialized Medical Center
@EdreesCenter
Send CV to: Exec.Admin@DrEdrees.com
تأسس 2006

This advert appeared on Facebook. Some countries such as the Middle East advertise for health professionals. While there are many attractive packages on offer, each applicant should take absolute care in checking the restrictions that might be in place

Overseas and work experience

Once you leave university at age 21-23 you have the world to explore. You have opportunities that allow you to travel and absorb experience. In the next few pages we can discover the case stories of several people who made decisions which had distinct benefits for their career development. Students should seek work experience wherever they can as this provides a quality medium to shape the future as well as providing value to their broader understanding.

A *curriculum vitae* built upon such experience can open the doors to career opportunities earlier. The reason for advancement and benefit is that managers and clinical leads can identify motivation and engagement.

Programmes

Overseas placements are not so common, but Huddersfield has established programmes with students going to Australia, New Zealand and Singapore. Other universities have followed.

> They've actually got jobs there with those practices afterwards. So that's been really exciting for those students, not just seeing what practice is like in the UK, but also overseas. we have lots of careers advisors who will do mock interviews, helping applications. **Grace Parfitt**

Grace developed different placements for students, some in the independent (private) sector. There is a keen acknowledgement that podiatry has become less NHS orientated and there is a need to ensure different exposure to various practices. Grace was a recipient of an excellent placement. As she studied at Huddersfield, she was fortunate to get on the ERASMUS programme. This was a European supported programme that sadly no longer exists since the UK came out of Europe.

As part of a 12-week final placement in Madrid she was able to share in one of the most exciting experiences dealing with diabetes and learning Spanish. A replacement for ERASMUS is promised and hopeful placements will not be limited to the UK alone. If you are lucky to have a good manager, funding can be found.

Silver Jubilee Award & Winston Churchill Fellowship Award
> My first two years, after graduating, were reinforced by a four month sabbatical studying musculoskeletal podiatry in the USA. The experience opened up teaching, orthotic manufacture, research, and offered an enduring network of friends and colleagues. **David Tollafield**

Kayron Pozo trained in the UK and works in Gibraltar. Podiatrists trained in the UK have either returned to their own countries such as Singapore, Hong Kong, Fiji, to name but a few, or have immigrated where their services are needed, often with limited competition but heaps of opportunity. Kayron's story is told in '*Voices from Podiatric Medicine*', the companion to this book.

Using basic orthotic skills to make off-loading insoles for leprosy sufferers.
Courtesy of Alison Clarke-Morris

Peripheral neuropathy & Leprosy

Leprosy, or Hansen's disease, is well known, just read any Christian bible. Being a leper led to being outcast from society. Heads were shrouded to protect country folk from seeing noses, eyes and other features distorted by the disease. The bacteria that causes the condition infects the nervous system and is interesting to the foot specialist for the reason that people cannot feel their feet.

The condition of leprosy provides exceptional exposure to the podiatrist's bag of skills. For those who wondered why they should spend hours learning scalpel skills, now the chance comes home to roost. Wound management is taken to new levels as lack of sensation produces trophic ulcers. Here are some stories from several experienced professionals who used their overseas experience to promote their career progress.

> It was a huge eye-opener to me as we had a fairly advanced practice. For example, if a bit of bone was sticking out of an ulcer, we would take that bit of bone away in the clinic. But it opened my eyes to what surgery could offer this patient group. And so, I knew from a relatively early age, within my surgical career, that was an area that I wanted to try and move into. **Ben Yates**

How does one get to go overseas?

Ben did not know it at the time, but he was adding a new skill. He left London to work overseas for 18 months, with six months spent in Calcutta, working for two large medical charities. He started working with surgeons, scrubbing in and assisting them with high-risk foot surgery.

> The Mother Teresa charity wrote back to me and said, "Yes, you're very welcome to come." I worked for them three days a week on the outskirts of Calcutta. **Ben Yates**

Ben would make insoles to offload pressure under the foot because people suffering from leprosy cannot feel their skin, which leads to damage. One can imagine treading on a sharp object without knowing it. The wound becomes infected and can travel up the leg without the patient realising that they are ill with the injury. Ben also worked out of Danang Hospital (Vietnam) covering clubfoot surgery in children, as well other abnormal deformities not generally seen in the West.

> I went to India with a rucksack, a suitcase full of sharp implements and a few donations of dressings and things, and ended up in Calcutta one morning working in a tent by the river. To be there one Monday morning, having never travelled out of Europe, was amazing really, having come from working in a very standard NHS community clinic. It was suddenly like the lightbulb went on, and I thought, this

is quite amazing that I've taken myself here, as a podiatrist. **Martin Fox**

Bible stories have inspired me. I felt quite a lot of sympathy for that group of people who were ostracised by their communities. At that point, I didn't know that they had foot ulceration. But learning about it at college I just thought, that's something I would really want to be able to do and help that community practically. I've always kept my eye open for opportunities, but never really been able to give up more than two-three weeks' time out of my working life because of various other constraints really, a bit family or financial. **Alison Clarke-Morris**

Skills building

While universities provide all graduates with a range of skills, it is not until employment begins that you know just how much or little you need to develop. We are all young once, and we believe we can fix the world, or so the saying goes. That drive, confidence and enthusiasm are what allow us to progress and adds knowledge that turns into a skill. Handling a sharp knife is second nature to every podiatrist.

Poor diet, poor hygiene, and lower castes are at greater risk from leprosy. Medieval images of people wearing sacks over their faces or hoods to minimise the visual effect of the disease are seen more in women than men in India. Women often lose their noses and try and hide them with their hands but their hands are probably worse than their noses because they often lose their fingers. Perhaps there is little humour to be found in such a profound condition.

Snapchat photography.
We were doing a lot more preventative care than we were on our wound care because they would come with a wound on one foot, and

we were insisting that they showed us the other foot. Pre-cleansing was important before we commenced working to remove dead tissue with a scalpel. I put a filter on my phone which gave her glasses, and it gave her a nose. And she was absolutely thrilled. She just couldn't stop looking at it. Women are more conscious than the men.
Alison Clarke-Morris

Our goal is to make the right decision. Training and learning will create the framework for us to grow with the seeds of motivation.

Planning does not always have to be written in' tablets of stone!'

Podiatry on the Move
Future aspirations

Desire to rehabilitate dancers

I haven't experienced much NHS podiatry. There are people prepared to pay and want to get better and want to do certain things, and I think you attract different kinds of people to different kinds of places. I would love to be able to help dancers and work with dance companies and elite ballet dancers. Their whole body does a lot, but their lower limb does so much, and I would love to be able to really get involved in that and help these dancers prevent injury as well as rehabilitate them. A lot of ballet dancers, especially male ballet dancers, have a lot of Achilles tendon problems. **Emily Reaney**

Two job offers

To be in my final year and have two job offers lined up for me before I graduated was something I could only have dreamt of really. One was the clinical demonstrator role at the university, which would have hopefully then led me down the academic route. The other one is a private practice down in Oldham. There's a pharmacist across the street that we work with, so medication is not a problem. He's also in contact with a podiatric surgeon. There is a vascular team with good connections to both the NHS and within the private sector. **Shuja Merban**

Shuja has the confidence of one of her tutors to consider becoming a university lecturer – clinical demonstrator, which she can carry out alongside her clinical work. And then there was the prospect of PhD. Clearly she has much to think about in her final year.

Governments make changes to Health Policy frequently and therefore what we consider relevant today might change tomorrow. At the time of writing, podiatry has a tremendous shortage of recruits. This places a student in a strong position and the NHS is likely to offer higher bands to graduates earlier, but this is not a guaranteed assumption.

Some university tutors feel students have sufficient experience to fill Band 6 and carry out many duties. The NHS is overloaded as anyone who reads the news knows. The pandemic has swept away much of a structure that, even before Covid, had left it struggling. The independent sector has had to take up the slack.

> I find now that I have patients who will go to their NHS appointments, but because they can't have one, for example, every three months, they want to come and see us maybe for two appointments in between. So they'll see the NHS for their first one, and us for two in between. So our services are getting more and more clogged up with more of the acute people, and more of the people that would ordinarily have been seen by NHS. But also people are just thinking,
>
> *"Well, I can go private. I don't need to wait for the GP to refer me anymore. I don't want to wait nine months, don't want to wait six months. I want to be seen now."* **Claire Carr**

Independent practice has formed the bulk of delivery, and with a good business approach students will find many modern practices are engaging them. This subject will be considered further in *'scope and practice'* in **Section 3.**

Gender and diversity

We want everyone to feel comfortable at university without prejudice. Racial variations in the UK come from mixed parentage from many countries and like all occupations there is a strong move to ensure an inclusive course cohort.

Britain (or if you prefer, the UK) thrives upon the richness of an open society adopting different viewpoints. One would be disingenuous to ignore the fact that not all systems are courteous toward those seen as non-indigenous to the UK. To brush racism out is ignorant and yet to focus on this alone must not override the fact that many have made high ranks and had success in their career.

Podiatry is not perfect, but it is better than many occupations that still struggle to smooth out gender and diversity issues. Language and foreign accents can present discrimination. Here is one example.

> I had a couple of bullying types of behaviour in uni towards me. That is like even in public when you go, people just assume Are you Polish? *"I'm like. You didn't even ask me where I came from. You just make a judgement because of the accent,"* so that's one of the things, but that is something you could come across anywhere you go. **Kersti Pedar** - *student*

Ganesh Baliah is a qualified podiatrist from Northampton University. Both his parents are Tamil, from South India. They were highly educated. Ganesh has no accent and admits he's embarrassed by his younger cousins who speak three or four languages very fluently, including English. He is sensitive to the current views about colour (BAME) and is actively interested in combatting discrimination.

> From a cultural viewpoint, it is more of a scientific degree programme. And certainly, looking at data and stats now for AHP professions, the BAME or minority representation seems still not best, but is better in degree programmes like podiatry. **Ganesh Baliah** – *independent podiatrist*

Britain is a multi-denominational and racially integrated society and our patients are as diverse as anywhere. All professions have challenges - the most significant challenge comes from identifying medical conditions among certain ethnic groups. All students must understand the importance of a balanced society and embrace the rich nature that university can offer without prejudice. Dealing with patients from mixed groups is both challenging and exciting.

> Research shows that one in three people will be of a colour in 20 years. How are we preparing our students for that in the future? It is about drivers representating medical bias. **Jill Halstead-Rastrick** - *research podiatrist special interest in social aspects of diversity & equality*

> Thankfully there were no bad experiences on my course, however, there are concerns from some that there aren't enough individuals from a BAME background in training – the reasons of which are multifactorial. **Usamah Khalid** – *trainee podiatrist in surgery*

Course Education Costs

Much has changed with respect to funding for students entering university, especially since the Tony Blair premiership. No publication can keep up with sudden shifts in government policy, but students obviously need to know how much their education will cost.

Podiatry is both vocational and academic. It has enjoyed bursaries and of course the standard university loans. Each part of the UK works differently, and depending upon where you live and your age – presumably school leaving age – there are other schemes that have come along which are attractive – these are called 'apprenticeship schemes' – *see after course education costs*.

NORTHERN IRELAND

'There is going to be a significant shortage of podiatrists.' However, Northern Ireland is not alone as recruitment has not produced the numbers required to meet manpower requirements in the NHS. There has never been a better time to train and find a job. This evidence has been presented by Health Education England.

> In Northern Ireland, student fees are commissioned by the Department of Health to fund places on Allied Health Professions courses. The fees in Northern Ireland are lower than in England, Wales and Scotland. The annual fee for an undergraduate course in Northern Ireland is about £3,600. There are limits on numbers set by the Department. Sometimes successful applicant numbers can rise a little over the number of funded places if they meet the criteria across the different health courses. **Raymond Robinson**

SCOTLAND

In Scotland, an undergraduate degree is effectively free for students from Scotland and the EU. This is thanks to a subsidy from the Student Awards Agency for Scotland (SAAS). The SAAS also offers a tuition fee loan of up to £5,500 for home postgraduate students.

It should be noted that the Scottish definition of "home" student differs slightly, in that it doesn't include students from the rest of the UK – i.e. England, Wales or Northern Ireland. Students from the rest of the UK who want to undertake an undergraduate degree in Scotland will pay up to £9,250 a year.

From an advantageous perspective, the additional fourth year does give the students that extra year to mature, to gain a good degree of clinical decision making and diagnostic skills. The disadvantage is that it costs another year of funding, although in Scotland the Scottish government pays all student fees.

> The student doesn't have an outlay of £9500 or so as you have in England, but you have an extra year of funding. And as a parent, you're funding a flat and the social aspects of being a student can be quite expensive. We sometimes get English students coming prior to having to pay in England, and one of the things that they would say is that extra year did give them the opportunity to have a longer summer holiday, which they could then work, and over the summer holidays build up some finances to help them with the following year. So there are advantages and there are disadvantages of that extra year. I've got some friends who studied down in London and they tell me they're getting quite a big debt after studying in university. I have some student loans, but I don't think it's at the same level. In Scotland you get free education, higher education, I've been to university before going to China, so I wasn't entitled to the free education. I didn't pay £1800 a year. It's not a lot, but funnily enough I was able to apply to the Carnegie Fund, and they're funding me for the course. And there's been lots of extra financial support through the pandemic as well. Recently there was a government funded grant I applied to and got money. We're quite lucky up here as far as the further education funding. **Paul Murphy**

WALES

Students from Wales pay £3,900 per year in UK tuition fees to study *anywhere* in the UK, with the rest covered by the Welsh government.

ENGLAND

The cost is £9,250 for students. The following information comes from QS TopUniversities (accessed May 2022)

https://www.topuniversities.com/student-info/student-finance/how-much-does-it-cost-study-uk

> UK students are eligible for loans, grants and other forms of funding to cover their UK tuition fees, with differing amounts of funding depending on location. While student loans for home students tend to cover all tuition fees, the additional loan to cover the cost of living in the UK often falls short of the amount actually needed. In the 2017/18 academic year, the maximum living loan was UK£8,430 for students outside London and up to £11,002 (~US$15,500) for those who study in London. In both cases, this is likely to be a few thousand pounds short of your annual living expenses.
>
> A large range of scholarships to study in the UK are also offered by the government, individual universities, independent organisations and various charities. The Education UK website [https://study-uk.britishcouncil.org/scholarships] provides an overview of scholarships available from the British Council and other organisations. It is also worth checking to see what scholarships and support schemes are available from the government and other organisations in your own country.

Overseas students should check the relevant UK Government sites as there are too many changes at present to publish any definitive costs. Universities will also assist in guiding students from overseas.

Changes can be expected with time because of the agreements between the E.U and the UK.

The Apprenticeship Scheme

This scheme is now being advertised by many NHS Trusts supported by universities offering another route to training while earning. Pay is lower but you are assured of a job with conditions. The Royal College of Podiatry website has published information – the link is [https://rcpod.org.uk/become-a-podiatrist/blog/podiatry-apprenticeship].

The NHS site https://www.stepintothenhs.nhs.uk also offers information.

Shona Wesley is now in her second year at Huddersfield University and engaging with more hands-on practice. Her confidence has grown with patients and she is comfortable working with the instruments at her disposal. She likes managing dermatological conditions, wound care and performing local anaesthetic blocks.

> When we're actually in university, there is no separation between the apprentice students and the other students. Everyone gets on as normal. Everyone mixes. There's no separation. It's not like that at all. So I feel like I've got the best of both worlds with it. **Shona Wesley**

She joined the apprenticeship scheme which offers students funded

A Career in Podiatric Medicine

placements where they have been engaged in other courses or have delayed entry to education. As a young person she feels at the age of 20 this has really helped. Funding comes from the apprenticeship scheme and the student works in the NHS and is paid alongside studying at university. Shona is currently paid as a Band 3. On qualifying she will go up to a Band 5. The system, at the time of writing has started to take off.

> There's just four of us. I think there are people doing it down in Brighton University, but this is the very first time this apprenticeship has ever been done as far as I know. Having left school I took a year out working in a dental practice because I didn't actually know what I wanted to do. It took me 12 months to work it out. I just earned a little bit of money and kind of got through with that. And I decided I wanted to study something in healthcare. I picked my subjects, I did them for two years and at the end I was still like, *"Well, I know I want to work in healthcare, but I'm still a little bit unsure which area."*
>
> So I looked into midwifery, I looked into nursing, and we had events at the college for careers, and different universities would come in and speak about their parts. There were things about medicine, dentistry, nursing, midwifery, law, police, but podiatry was never mentioned and I didn't even know it was a thing. It's not something I've ever come into contact with at all. I went to Salford University just before my final 'A' Levels and I had a look around, primarily to scout out nursing. However, while I was there the podiatry department was just across the way. So I thought, *"Oh, what's that like? I don't even know what that is. So I thought, I'm going to go and have a look."* I got speaking to some people and they explained about a career in podiatry. I came across an apprenticeship in podiatry that was being advertised in the East Lancashire NHS Trust. I got a phone call to go for an interview. I had to make a presentation about why I should get the job, and at this point I knew hardly anything about podiatry so I spent a long time putting that together. I went for the and I got a phone call later that day saying, *"Do I want the job?"*
>
> The course is still a full-time degree but three days a week. Because of how much extra studying there is, this is the one downside I would say with this apprenticeship. You have to work hard. But it's completely worth it.

When students are on holiday she carries on working because of the apprenticeship contract.

Modern university libraries allow you to have books as well as journals on line

Books & Journals

Students are thrifty when it comes to purchasing books, of which there are plenty. Universities are equipped with fantastic library services and many materials, including books, can be borrowed electronically.

Books

Buying books second hand is also another common trend so the first-year user might receive a great deal from a final year student wishing to cash in. Join podiatry Facebook sites (*e.g UK Podiatry*) where you might see practitioners selling off books at reasonable prices.

Amazon and Abe Books provide two useful sites where second handbooks can be sold relatively cheaply, but look at the cost of something new first before agreeing a second-hand purchase. The downside with books can be their content might be out of date.

Journals

Journals provide current thought but have a narrower viewpoint than books. They are specific and in most cases will report work within the last three to five years around any particular subject. Access to journals from university libraries make this a strong resource, and any visit to a university should include a trip to the library and resource centre. It is important to bear in mind most assignments require strong references.

Official journals have a specific order of presentation specified by each editorial responsible for selecting material. The stronger journals have high citation rates, meaning that they attract heavy readership from which work is quoted. Over recent years journals are the go to place but with so many publications the ability to read everything is not possible. Most clinicians are selective in what they read to prioritise their time.

Students are encouraged to submit articles early in their career but a word of warning, avoid paying to have your article in a journal as the peer review process may not be as robust. Always seek advice from your tutor in this regard.

- Visit at least one practice in the independent sector and one in the NHS (*Google or go to the RCoP site to find a podiatrist*)
- Read literature or books about podiatry
- Look at websites (*universities and local practices*)
- Check out the main professional body's websites (*see end of book*)
- Attend a university open day
- When you visit anywhere have your C.V. to hand
- Write down your course preferences based on your research
- Form a list of strengths and weaknesses, opportunities and drawbacks
- Consider how far you wish to be located from home
- Look at accommodation & travel flexibility and costs

Kick starting your career with choice

4 - Podiatrists Serving the Nation's Foot Health

Most podiatrists are great at essential clinical work, some might call it routine, and don't necessarily wish to specialise at the top level. However, most find that their days are anything but routine. There is always something new, all patients are different - *"life is like a box of chocolates!"* (Forest Gump)

Should you work in the NHS or in other sectors? *This is for you to decide!*

In **Section 4** you will find a clearer concept of general practice in podiatry. I will also dip into some areas of special interest. Health screening does not just involve the foot. I will consider the scope of work, career planning and progression as well as look at the meaning of caseload. Understanding current specialist practices together with high-risk patients allows us to appreciate how each area of podiatry varies for different types of patient. Last, what do we mean *Core Podiatry*?

Where do you start?

Upon graduating, most students select independent practice or head for the NHS. There are other routes other than the NHS such as 'Sole Trader' within independent practice. Sole Trader is a term used when you are self-employed outside a company, so therefore you are treated as single person business as opposed to being *limited* (Ltd.). The term independent practice is used interchangeably with private practice.

You might join a locum agency as well as work for larger foot health or footwear companies. If you want to stay near your family home your choice in the NHS may be limited and the career progression slower. Competition for the roles in MSK, nail surgery, children's podiatry are examples of specialisation that all students head for – *I know, I did this over 40 years ago and things don't change.* You do have to work your time though, walk not run.

Most students look for full-time work, while mature students, with families, view employment differently. Each placement at university will offer the undergraduate a different experience. Career progression in the NHS is better when you have a solid grounding. Managers often feel more attracted to invest in staff who have put their time in. Most of us take six months to two years to feel confident - learning the ropes, but then it depends on placements and personal experience.

Explaining General Podiatry

It may appear confusing to see the term *'general'* which implies that the scope of practice is not limited. The General Practitioner in Podiatry (GPP) may offer a wide range of services but may also have a sub-specialty interest. The general practitioner might work in both the independent (private) sector or in the NHS.

We know what a GP does in medicine and we know what a dentist does. We also know doctors and dentists work in hospitals and provide different services. In the same way the podiatrist functions as a general practitioner. If you come into the profession of podiatry today I will guarantee that it will have changed within 10 years, if not faster.

The author demonstrates the smokelyzer which measures carbon dioxide.
Smoking affects circulation to the limbs and feet

First line contact & screening

The medical GP is a first-line practitioner but this assumption is changing, and the advent of the Covid-19 pandemic has accelerated change. The GP was the first clinician to see a life-threatening problem – cancer of the skin, impending foot gangrene or early infection.

Today any healthcare professional might see changes in their patient that need alerting and this is where GPPs form a valuable radar for the healthcare system link to the GP in medicine by providing an important screening role.

The general podiatry practitioner might offer a wide service. Screening involves examining and testing; blood pressure, urine, weight, smoking, neurological and circulation checks, signs of skin deterioration, blemishes, swellings, reduced joint movement, loss of muscle power are key indicators for concern. Smoke checks can be made using a small breathalyser (pictured) that measure expired carbon monoxide.

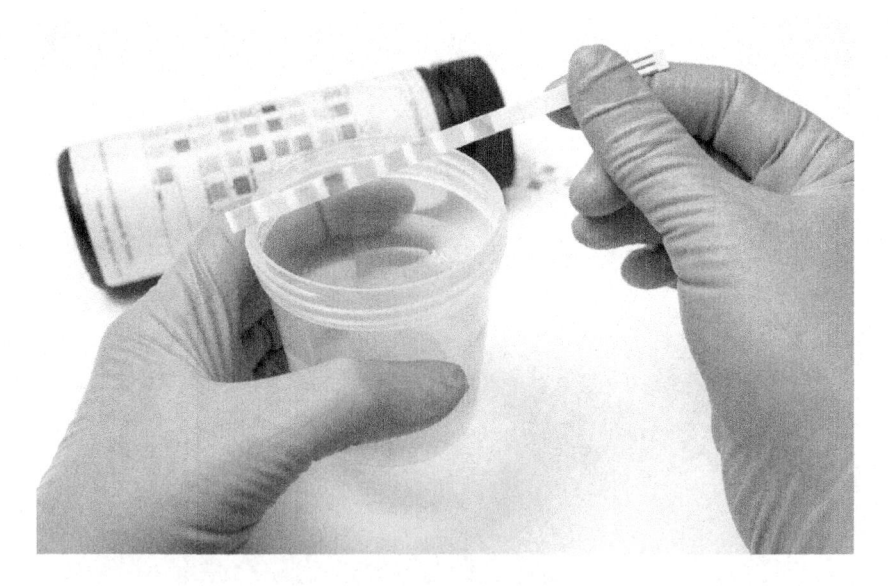

Testing urine may appear unpleasant, but it is the most common method of screening for early diseases of the kidney and pancreas (glucose control). We can tell if someone is dehydrated, to having a water infection, providing advice as to why a wound might not have healed.

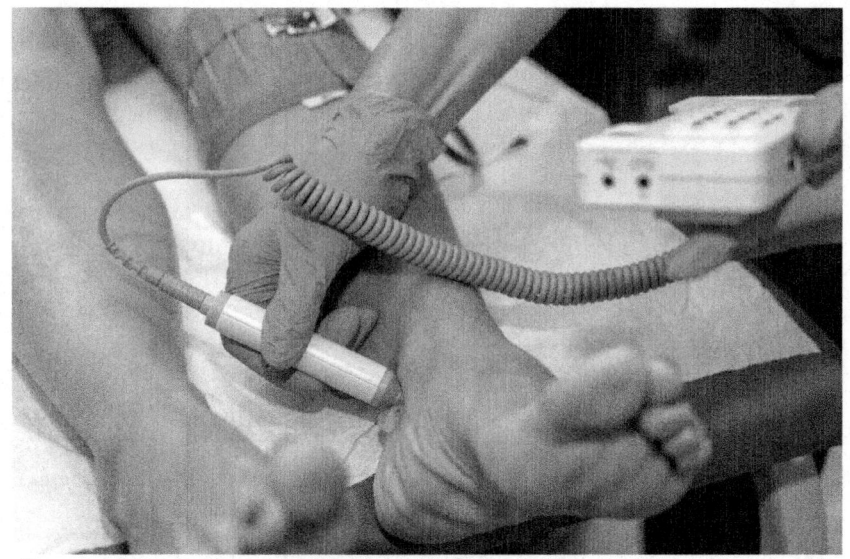

The Doppler (shown above) is a hand-held device to listen to blood flow. In this picture, the podiatrist is identifying flow in one of the key arteries in the foot.

What we do and what we would like to do

In a career book it would be wrong to suggest how to set up practice as the content is really about what you might expect and whether the career, in this case podiatry, has an attraction for a school leaver or a mature graduate. By knowing what lies ahead - and believe me those discussing their role in podiatry know their stuff - you will gain a better insight about the possibilities. More information is covered in developing a career plan in this section. Most podiatrists sub-specialise in one subject or other.

Sub-specialising

> I was a generalist in podiatric surgery, but had a strong interest in pain management, rheumatology and pathology. In the latter case, pathology meant studying microbiology and histology. I built a large catalogue of histology samples. It's not just about the condition that you are treating but understanding what happens at a deeper level in the foot. In time this meant as sure as night follows day – I was going to find malignancy. Having a great team of physicians such as oncologists and plastic surgeons around allowed us to do some amazing things and save lives through early intervention. I thanked my abilities that I could undertake surgery at any level to help my patients – **David Tollafield**

Intimacy and emotion

> When I was a student, the first moment when you're practicing on each other, and they have to take their shoes and socks off in

front of a stranger, there is this realisation that your feet are a really intimate part of your body. People can be intensely private about their feet. And, if they have a problem with their feet, it's almost magnified. It can be a really genuinely emotional moment. **Siobhan Muirhead**

Treatment commences with careful history taking.
Patients are not just an NHS number but a human being. It is important with so many different factors to consider, you have to provide the right health promotion. Taking a good clinical history before you start your hands-on check is really important - say they're a diabetic, checking circulation is essential, maybe there is an open skin wound - this is about preventative measures to stop ulceration, gangrene and a possible amputation. You could really spend all day just trying to tell them what is right or what is wrong in terms of wealth of professional opinion and advice on footwear, changing their diet, taking exercise and making them aware of their general health. **Shuja Merban**

So much of what we do is based around our contact with people and using their information productively, but much comes down to communication and listening to what patients want before we tell them what they need.

Making a Career Plan

We all need a career plan, hence placements and secondments are important when trying to find a niche early in your career. Being employed provides security for many. Building confidence first before going solo is often advocated for some, but not all. It is a time of great excitement as you are now free from having to ask every time you need to take action. Adopting a mentor, a senior person who has some experience, is important. In the NHS look for an AfC Band 6 podiatrist or seek out a buddy-partner if you join a practice.

Networking

Join a professional body that provides indemnity cover. Sign-up to one of the big conferences as soon as you can and start to network. There are people from all over the UK and abroad who attend these events and can provide you with a wealth of knowledge.

You will need a membership journal to stay in touch with on-going courses on offer as well as complying with something called continuous professional development (CPD). E-newsfeeds are worth subscribing to. Podiatrists are expected to keep up to date and show how they are doing so. This is similarly expected of all registered healthcare professionals. A local regional group or local branch allows you to learn from experienced colleagues. This helps pick up information about an unfamiliar area; what to avoid and what to get stuck into.

The NHS provides mandatory in-service courses which cover a ton of different policies. In the independent sector the induction is more laid back unless you elect to work for a company or private hospital which will require policies to be followed and an induction to meet their insurance requirements.

Students should have a rough idea where they want to work and which type of work they might wish to engage with.

MSK & Nail surgery
> I would probably like to get into the NHS for a couple of years' experience. But I think I'm actually going to go down the private practice route. I've had a few job offers to work as an associate whenever I do graduate. And someday hopefully, I would love to own my own practice - I will probably focus on the MSK side of things and nail surgery. **Paul Haughian**

Mixing wound care and MSK
> When I've qualified, I'm going to start as a Band 5 but definitely want to progress as much as I can. I've got a strong interest in the wound care side of things now I've been working with diabetic patients and with wounds and things like that and helping to care for them and experimenting with the different dressings and things like that and watching them improve. That's really rewarding. I have been getting into the MSK side of things as well. I do really like the idea of doing some biomechanics, but I'm just going see what happens really. I'd love to be an AfC Band 7 or something one day. That would just be fantastic. **Shona Wesley**

What does a General Practitioner in Podiatry Do?

Everything!

Of course you won't have the experience to care for every patient when you qualify. In fact, it is likely you will never ever have all the experience you might desire. None of us knows everything and we learn something new every day. Every foot disorder is accompanied by other concerns and this is where we have to apply a holistic approach. 'Holistic' means that a problem is wider than an isolated part. You cannot look at a foot and ignore the rest of the body.

Learning to deal with people is the hard bit because not everyone comes to you with the kindness or view that you are new. You carry the title podiatrist and therefore are expected to know!

> By now you realise that there is a fair bit of general work. You will meet hard skin and nails. Some podiatrists have little to do with this part of our role, others thrive. By the time I was practising as a foot surgeon, a little bit of regular nail management acted as a welcome respite. My patient had been fighting cancer and the drugs had damaged her nail plate. Her oncologist (*cancer specialist*) sent her to me when in fact any general podiatrist would have been fine. I looked after her for years until finally the cancer came back. **David Tollafield**

Your job is to seek information, work a diagnosis, provide a cause (aetiology), and set out a management plan. If the patient does not want to go further then you need an alternative strategy. If the patient has a problem that you cannot treat, it is your job to find a person who can help.

> I love speaking to podiatrists working in general practice. The treatment plan doesn't just stop with conservative treatment - there is the option of surgery and it's very much their role to advise the patient about surgery. And as such, they should be informed upon the risks and complications of surgery as well as the successful outcomes associated with surgery. That is their role. **Tim Kilmartin**

Put bluntly - know when to refer and know who to refer to and give them the correct advice. You don't have to be a qualified surgeon to help a patient.

The Softer Side of Podiatry

Podiatry provides an element of aesthetic delivery in feet, but this is always takes the medical perspective into consideration. Foot Health Practitioners (FHP) overlap with some of this activity, but they are not podiatrists. Correspondence and block courses are run by the SMAE Institute, who have been training people in foot care since the start of the 20th century. FHPs are trained to know when to pass certain patient groups on to qualified podiatrists.

Judith entered the university course as a mature professional, and can now expand her range of activities that before were out of her reach. FHPs deal with low-risk patients and provide an excellent service in keeping their feet comfortable. Judith wanted to use modern diagnostic techniques, treat a local football team, use local anaesthetics and apply musculoskeletal studies at a level that could help her patients.

> I was so frustrated as an FHP because there were so many things I didn't know and I wanted to know and so many times I'd have to refer people on to somebody else, to a podiatrist, and I thought, "Oh, I wish I could do that." We can only deal with low risk, just maybe prevention, so it doesn't go into immediate risk. When people come in and say, "I've got a sore ankle, I want to know what that is. I want to be able to help. I want to be able to fix you." If I'm seeing somebody with maybe cellulitis, I panic. I go, "Please go and see your GP." I always felt I don't know enough. So there's definitely a difference between FHPs and podiatrists. They're absolutely not the same. Podiatrists are more than nail cutters and hard skin removers because that's what I am (as a former FHP). I'm a nail cutter. I'm a hard skin remover. **Judith Watson,** *former student & registered nurse, University of Ulster.*

Many students seeking podiatry were often given the impression that the profession was about cutting toe nails and trimming corns, only to find out that entering a three or four-year degree reading podiatric medicine was very different.

The NHS does not provide 'pedicure' emphasising high-risk cases, a point repeated in this book. All podiatrists learn how to reduce callus and enucleate corns for one purpose. We can extend this principle to the nails as well. There is an intense degree of skill and hours required to use a scalpel. The purpose is to decipher the underlying tissue from healthy to necrotic, from inflamed to malignant tissue.

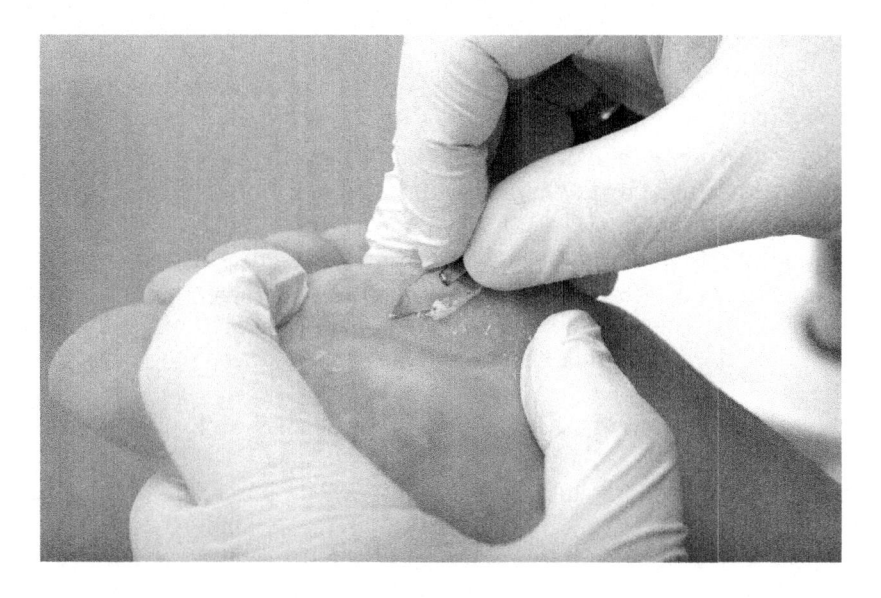

Superficial debridement is shown using a scalpel designed to identify the condition of the underlying skin. This is partly diagnostic but does offer the patient relief. This skill requires plenty of clinical exposure as everyone's skin (tissue) is different

A Common Feature in Feet

There are common conditions that comprise a proportion of the generalist's case load. The musculoskeletal (MSK) element deals with connective tissue damage, strains and deeper changes in the foot and joints.

When it comes to skin - callus and corns occur in different degrees and can form extremely painful conditions from splitting skin (fissures) to deeper ulcers, foreign indwelling damage and cysts. The nail bed harbours many problems and requires skill to navigate fleshy tumours and overgrown blood vessels causing deformity and distortion known as hypergranulation.

Because the foot contacts the ground, it is exposed to injury. Friction blisters alert us to pain but many problems remain locked away from the eye unless pain breaks through. The podiatrist must understand dermatology - medicine associated with the skin and pathology, to be able to debride with skill and create no harm.

While many adverts talk about the three conditions – corns, callus and nails, they seldom point out why podiatrists have to become heavily skilled. Qualified Doctor of Medicine in dermatology often defer to podiatrists, including the common infection called the foot wart (Greek – verruca pedis) caused by the human papillomavirus.

In addition, we treat dermatophytic infections (fungal or mycotic forms) that affect skin and nails. Microbiology is taught within pathology in years 1 and 2. Infections around the nail are increasingly treated by podiatrists who have led the field of healthcare with proven success.

Treatment for corns and callus requires knowledge of locally applied medication, the use of diagnostic imaging such as ultrasound, sample biopsy to rule out malignancy, cultures for infections, detailed medical history to rule out other skin diseases, and underlying medical conditions. The use of caustics and keratolytics may be used, or cryotherapy, electrical desiccation, microwave and laser to produce controlled destruction of abnormal blood vessel changes in skin. Surgical excision and plastic skin flap surgery have their place, but are outside the undergraduate training programme.

If there is a soft side of podiatry, the harder side is based around biomechanics – physical forces applied to the human body. Many podiatrists find this area of work attractive, not least because it is full of new exciting gizmos, and various measuring systems. Student Zoe provides an example.

Managing tendo-achilles problems (tendinopathy.
> After careful questioning it turned out that the patient had started a new job and the cause was occupational. Once a working cause can be found I would set out to manage the root cause, and change certain aspects of the patient's daily routine. **Zoe Alexander**

Ultrasound scanning is now part of the investigations introduced into many regular podiatry clinics as well as using force plates to measure foot pressures during walking linked to computers. Video playback is a common tool used in clinics, often based around treadmills. All of this forms part of gait (walking) analysis.

The Clinic and Caseload

Assistants can keep stock inventory and support you in managing your caseload – *the name for patient lists*. We have to keep good records and communicate with other agencies. Advising a district nurse, GP or hospital consultant about their patient improves integrated care.

The computer is standard for clinics; from management to appointments to providing information and linking electronic records to other health agencies. Most NHS services rely on computers and access to laboratory results. X-rays now offer a wide range of information and can be viewed on the screen allowing patients to see the results.

NHS clinics meet set standards in health centre rooms in the community. Some clinics in hospitals may share consulting rooms with other teams. In the private sector a good practice will invest in the most modern equipment, including examination chairs which often look like dental chairs. Autoclaves maintain instrument sterilisation although some people prefer pre-packed sterilised instruments. Your course will have provided all the information to maintain the highest standards of hygiene for procedures.

Practices may share facilities with various professionals as seen in the case of Afni Shah-Hamilton, i.e. sharing dental suites. Some podiatrists work with physiotherapists, chiropractors and osteopaths. The large passage of through clientele attract people to purchase their healthcare in one location. For many years, GP surgeries, which incidentally are not owned by the NHS, form a business partnership with other GPs. Empty rooms will always attract clinicians from other disciplines. Utilisation and potential income for these practices makes business attractive to part-time users.

Podiatrists have access to a range of medicines, which may be provided via the NHS budget, thus reducing the need to seek GP's provision for such drugs as antibiotics and pain medication. Non-medical or independent prescribing (I.P.) is more accessible today and a new graduate will want to consider if they have access through their employment or need to go on a course. In some cases clinicians may feel they do not need I.P. unless they are working at a higher level of risk.

There is no age range in the independent sector. You will treat babies to the most elderly. The NHS has stricter criteria and as this is constantly changing. New graduates will need to check out local policies. One of the most interesting aspects of working for yourself in the private sector is that you can choose your hours of work as well as see a wide range of conditions across all the age groups. As graduates become more comfortable with their new environment, it is natural to seek out areas of special interest.

Injectable treatment

All podiatrists can perform standard anaesthetic blocks for toes, and in some cases perform more advanced blocks to anaesthetise the whole foot for electrocautery, cryosurgery, deeper excisions of skin, biopsy (where trained) and nail removal in sections or whole nails. Those who have been mentored will perform a variety of other injections which may include steroids. The use of water-based and glucose-based (prolotherapy) substances may also be used for joints and tendons. The most recent changes to independent practice have included the use of ultrasound to aid diagnosis, but training is required to be able to perform this type of interpretation.

A Career in Podiatric Medicine

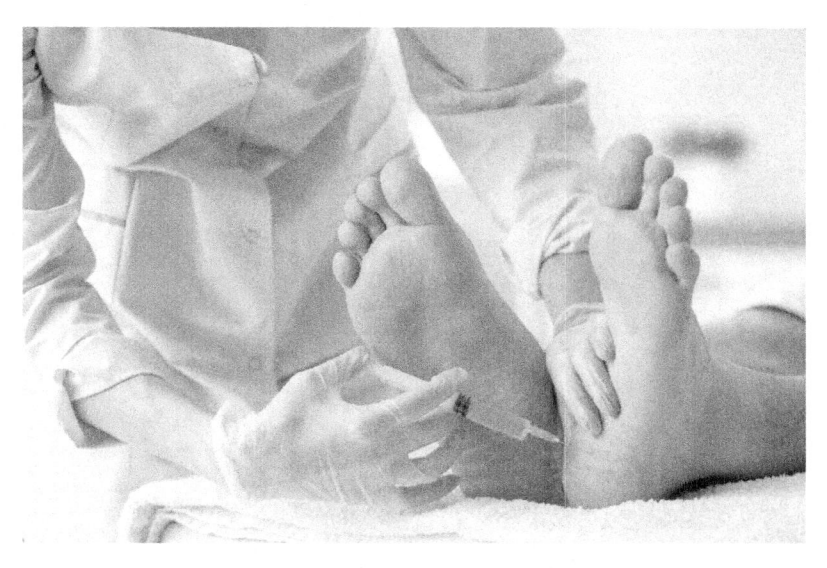

Essential musculoskeletal science skills, studying biomechanics and insoles form a large part of private practice involving some form of rehabilitation with exercises, dressings, dynamic taping, and custom-made orthoses made to a prescription taken from a plaster cast or scanner.

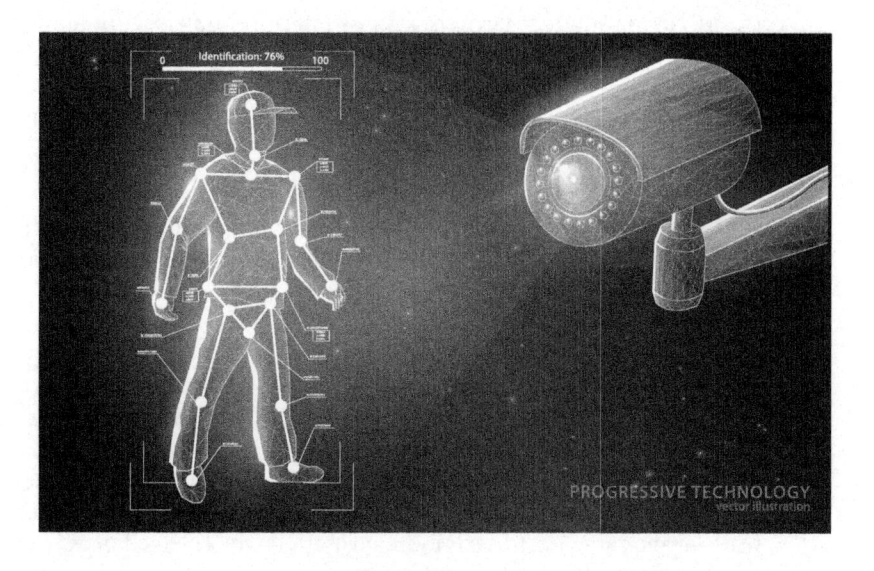

Gait analysis involving video recording, walkways, treadmills and pressure measuring platforms are part of the independent sector's skill set, but are less common in the podiatric NHS sector

The explosion of running for charities has made people more aware of foot function

Sports people appear in clinics in greater numbers as podiatrists have taken an interest in human motion studies related to feet. Getting involved with fun runs and helping runners with strains, swellings, blisters and wounds can only enhance practice. Growing numbers of podiatrists are using tools such as a dermatoscope to spot cancers on feet. You may wonder why we manage nails – well, malignancy can be found under the nail plate and can lead to early death. Cancers in feet are being missed because of the lack of face-to-face examination in medical practices as well as knowledge over common skin problems. Podiatrists may pick up contract work with various community groups such as residential homes or go to prisons to perform a number of sessions. With the right enthusiasm any graduate can develop additional worthwhile skills within a short period of time.

> In order to deliver podiatric care in some rural parts of Scotland telemedicine is being used. As an example, the multi-disciplinary diabetes team in Inverness use telemedicine to provide diabetes consultations on some of the most rural areas and remote islands within the Health Board. There are so many new and different methods of treatment available which can only enhance patient care while at the same time being more cost effective. Telemedicine is a great example of how patient management has changed. **Stuart Baird**

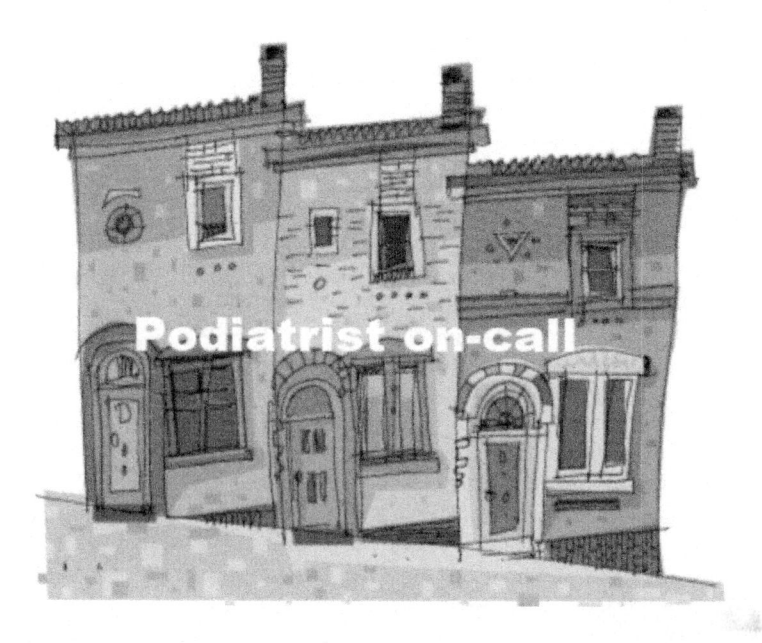

The Home Visit

Most practices will offer some home visits. These can be fun and allow you to get out of clinic. The NHS podiatry service has shrunk this option so much that anyone entitled to a house call almost certainly has to use the independent sector if not just to improve the frequency of visits. But this is not always the case and the NHS maintains a focus on high risk.

> We still do domiciliaries. We don't do anything low risk or what's classed as social nailcare and we don't do any patient that is not bed bound/house bound. So if you can mobilise from bed to a chair, okay, but if you can mobilise around the house independently or could go out, if somebody could pick you up to drive you, then no, you have to come back into clinic. I'm quite strict on that because domiciliary treatment can be a back breaker. So I do push people back into clinic when it's appropriate.
>
> We had a poor person that I went to go and see. I was taking a new AfC Band 5 around and showing him the ropes, and I said, "Go on, you can do this one. You're fine, you can crack on. It's just two apical wounds. It'll be alright." He took one plaster off and I went – "Oh, it's osteomyelitis almost certainly." **Sarah Twiss**

Maintaining healthy feet in the older population involves screening for early problems associated with poor healing and blood flow. Secondly, podiatry maintains mobility which equates to a healthier life. Domiciliary care is part of practice visiting people in their home, in their own domestic setting. Care homes may be included in a visiting practice.

> Within the domiciliary practice you deal more with mental health issues and health institutions, and supported living environments. I've been into homes with adult learning difficulties. I've seen people who normally attend clinic who've maybe fallen over, broken their hip and they can't get back to the clinics. I've seen them at home to provide continuity of care. There's the added bonus of this trusted individual who they're welcoming into their home. Patients who cannot reach clinic need our help to retain as much mobility as possible and to keep them pain free. You might be the first person in a wider healthcare team that actually recognised that this person has problems because they're sleeping in a chair rather than a bed. No two days are the same. There is a different connection with somebody when you're going into their home compared to someone attending clinic. **Louise Kennedy**

> You may visit a farm one day, or a nursing home another. Flats, semis, cottages, tower rise flats and on one occasion I had visited a patient in a converted windmill. There is poverty and privilege, but you have to learn not to judge. **David Tollafield**

As Louise points out, when we see a patient in their natural environment, we don't just see a patient but we can take on board how they live as well as identify more accurately with their social capacity, their movement and what they wear on their feet.

Podiatrists should be aware, as much as any health worker going into homes, to make a wider assessment beyond the immediate area of their own skill. In some ways the podiatrist adopts the role of social worker or even an occupational therapist through abstract observation.

The assessment of mobility is often more perceptive than in clinic. Trip hazards from carpets are one concern as painful hips mean feet cannot be raised to clear the smallest of steps. Patients are not always elderly but may be housebound or terminally ill, be stroke victims or suffer from multiple sclerosis. They're people who maybe have more complex health issues than you would see in clinic; that have hospital beds in their room and have carers who visit several times a day. All this makes the podiatrist's approach different to dealing with somebody who's in a clinical environment.

> When you see someone's home, they have photographs, and you learn about the person and you're talking to them while you're doing your job and making a genuine connection with that person. The fact that you go in and you'll be cheery faced, and that you're a trustworthy person, to make a visit can make a massive difference to somebody's day. So many elderly people are suffering from dementia, and they'll ask you 10 times if they've paid you and they hand you an envelope with £20 notes and say, *"take what you need."* I dread to think about somebody who isn't honest. So it's nice that you can go in and out and you feel that people had a safe person in their home. **Louise Kennedy**

The National Health Service
Scope and Practice

The NHS adopted bands based around Agenda for Change (AfC) from 2004, replacing the older Whitley Scale of payments. Podiatrists are employed from AfC Band 5 at graduation through to 8. Unless you commence higher skilled work, most podiatrists will reach AfC Band 7. Band 8-9 forms the top end and are not discussed under general practice. At the time of writing pay awards for 2022-3 were awaited. AfCBand 5 starts at £25,655 and goes through to AfC Band 7 after 4 years at £45,839. Compare these figured to foundation training for medical doctors who work longer hours; £29,384 - £34,012.

Some podiatrists find themselves with AfC Band 5 grades and feel limited in their ability. One of the most rapid changes within the NHS has been the establishment of the Extended Scope Practitioner. In truth many have participated in modules, courses and Master's degrees, while others have built their ability around being in practice for many years, accruing a wealth of knowledge.

Use of core skills

One of the things we try and do at Huddersfield with our undergraduates is get them to try and think for themselves to make clear decisions about treatment plans that make a difference to the patient. (We) try and emphasise that these are the professional standards of proficiency, conduct performance and ethics. Just because you're a Band 5, doesn't mean you can't do things, Okay, you might not want to do something because you haven't got the experience, and that's okay to refer on but actually, some of these things are actually things that you should be able to do. You know, even at a baseline level to start off the treatment rather than just saying automatically, *"Oh, it's got to be referred onto somebody higher."*

Being a Band 5 should not restrict your practice, the only thing that's lacking is experience. In the NHS we hear that Band 5's can't see new patients, nail surgery, MSK assessments, diabetic ulcer treatments etc. Yes they can, but they need help. **Andy Bridgen**

A Career in Podiatric Medicine

Adjustment or manufacture has always been a traditional manual skill for podiatrists

Orthoses and manufacture in the NHS
We mainly provide customised (casted) orthoses similar to the American model. Most podiatrists manufacture their own orthotics with or without the help of a technician. When I started to work in the UK, I was surprised by the number of over-the-counter orthoses that podiatrists prescribe, as I was taught to use cast - made to measure as the primary option in most cases. Having been in the UK a while, I realised there is no consensus or strong evidence on most of the techniques used in 'orthotics' and 'biomechanics'. **Rodrigo Diaz-Martinez**

Podiatry departments used to provide an in-house laboratory where each clinician might fabricate their own prescription for his or her patient. The NHS is a non-profit business and has restricted many practices once used, including home visits as a routine service for the housebound. Decisions are made around financial accountability.

The manufacture of orthoses has gone the same way as home visits, although a service can be found in patches. Orthotists (a separate professional) provide orthoses to contract. Podiatrists have found newer designs of orthoses are perceived as being more effective as modular systems. These are pre-prepared, high quality materials that can be manipulated in clinic, saving money and reducing the need for expensive laboratories fitted with safety equipment which requires maintenance.

Orthotic work in the independent sector is free from some of the limited resources imposed by the NHS as it is paid for directly by the patient or from private funding groups where patients pay money regularly into a health fund. The NHS still provides orthotic services free but this is likely to change.

The benefit of working for the NHS and some private organisations allow provision of statutory sick pay, holidays and pensions, but the salary and increments are fixed upon service conditions and meeting strict criteria.

Moving from AfC Band 5 to Band 6 is relatively fast but AfC Band 7+ may prove more difficult depending upon the type of work and skills adopted.

Career Ladder

While independent practice has no formal career pathway, the NHS does offer a graded ladder depending upon the type of specialisation that is attractive to the podiatrist

Moving Up the Ladder in the NHS

Postgraduate course funding may not always be provided and will depend on training budgets. Mandatory training such as life support, patient lifting and talks on child protection form a whole range of courses that have to be funded. The young podiatrist must get used to fighting their corner or bidding for a course having presented their case. This becomes no easier when the department has a number of motivated clinicians all vying for the same course or programme.

One way of improving your career potential is to be prepared to move from one Trust to another and seek out one of the four key groups where AfC band growth can occur. The other way is to become involved with in-service training; to become attached to one of these higher skilled podiatry units. The four areas below are common to *higher risk patients*.

- MSK triage work with orthopaedics as an extended scope practitioner
- Work within rehabilitation using MSK and general skills e.g rheumatology
- Diabetes and high-risk vascular care
- Podiatric surgery

Each of these NHS specialties will form a longer career choice leading to higher band at AfC grading i.e Bands 7-8. AfC Band 8 is divided into a-d so in effect mini-bands within a major band. Current salaries start from £47,126 (a) - £78,192 (d) and AfC Band 9 £93,735 – £108,075. More information can be found via the NHS website under Section 6 (salaries in the NHS).

Openings to each specialty may be limited and sometimes podiatrists are best to seek study leave release to show motivation, even if it is within the same Trust. We live in a society today where some say that we are owed a living. Any young graduate who wants career progression should dismiss this idea as pure bunkum. Be prepared to work longer hours and sometimes for little monetary gain if you want to reach the echelons of higher positions. Working in the independent sector is no different – no pain, no gain!

Extended Scope Practitioners

ESP grades have been around for some years and cover more advanced NHS work. Here I will cover the musculoskeletal group part of ICATS. The title is also given the abbreviation MICATS. Vascular and diabetes as well as surgery will be covered under this heading.

Integrated Clinical Assessment and Treatment Services (ICATS)

This group starts at AfC Band 7 although Edwina Alcock is on NHS Band 8a. She is an Extended Scope Practitioner working within MICATS.

Physiotherapy has led the ESP initiative, and now APP – advanced practitioner in physiotherapy or podiatry. Many podiatrists have been employed to provide orthotic services, injection therapy, and provide imaging to screen patients. In addition to working within the MSK framework, Musculoskeletal Clinical Assessment and Treatment services (MICATS) forms part of a team approach.

Students who study biomechanics and MSK at university should appreciate that if they wish for a NHS career in this area the development of MSK is forever changing. Edwina Alcock built her career up from a new concept post, using bolt on modules and courses. She had to take the IRMER qualification to allow her to access radiology services. An advert is included below for an ESP post demonstrating a typical pre-requisite for an applicant. Because Edwina joined when ESPs-ICATS was new she has seen changes and developments over the years as well as appreciating the benefit to her patients and the support available with physiotherapy.

> My role is to work within a team of advanced practitioner physiotherapists as part of muscular skeletal and pain management. That's our group and team. We will assess all our patients – not just feet specialising in biomechanics; injection, investigations might be part of that. So we will try and exhaust everything for that patient before we make decisions on surgery with them. We also shadow and have good relationships with local surgeons. It's a bit of a one-stop shop where we use all those skills to treat that patient, but we are to say to one of the physios, *"can you come and have a look at Mrs. Jones with me? She's got a positive tendinopathy. If I book her with you, can you do this, this and this- and it's done."* We also are able

to send them to orthotics. We may make a chairside appliance for them first and if they have a really good result, we'll send them to the orthotist. And we've also offer a pain management service. It's a real integrated team work. **Edwina Alcock**

Edwina has reached a point in her career where she is now part-time but mentors podiatrists wishing to come into the APP/ESP field of practice.

> Every day is a school day, and it's really a great place to be, looking at patients with foot and ankle pain, but also looking at patients with lower back pain.

NHS ADVERT FOR MSK PODIATRY CLINICAL POSITION

The NHS advert is real but has been edited from a website [24/4/2022] to show the type of work being advertised. The podiatrist has to have additional musculoskeletal abilities. The Trust title has been replaced with [Name].

> We are looking for a highly motivated, enthusiastic podiatrist, with a proven track record in MSK, to join our team. The post is a part time (23 hours per week) MSK Podiatry clinical position. (Name) Podiatry department provide MSK Podiatry services across (Name) in a number of different clinical sites, based mainly in Community Hospitals. We have excellent links with the wider WHC multidisciplinary team, particularly physiotherapy. There is currently a large physiotherapy led MSK project on-going in (Name), with the formation of an Orthopaedic Interface Service staffed by extended scope practitioners. We work very closely with their team and regularly liaise regarding patient care as well as offer mutual peer support. We also have excellent links with a number of podiatric surgeons in the area with cross referral and regular communication commonplace.
>
> The MSK team have access to a range of treatments and protocols including diagnostic imaging requesting (subject to current IR(ME)R certification), prefabricated, customised and bespoke orthoses, as well as direct onward referral to many other disciplines if necessary.
>
> (Name) Health and Care Podiatry department as a whole, is a community based service concentrating on the treatment of 'at-risk' and 'high-risk' feet and musculoskeletal problems. We are a small, friendly team committed to staff development and training. We regularly undertake CPD activities and encourage each member of the team to participate and fulfil their own potential. We have a

regular clinical supervision programme and we actively encourage peer to peer support and learning.

The exact area that this post covers will be agreed with the successful applicant. There is a need to work at different clinical sites to provide care to MSK patients as required. The successful applicant will have a close working relationship with other Specialist Podiatrists within the organisation to ensure that key areas are delivered.

Extended scope podiatrist in podiatric orthopaedics

Damian Holdcroft started off taking some of the original courses to become a podiatric surgeon and then took a managerial route before returning to clinical practice in surgery, then later on with orthopaedic surgery. By undertaking some dual clinics with the consultant orthopaedic surgeon and lead in foot and ankle surgery, he developed his own unique ESP set up in an acute hospital.

There was no blueprint set out for an extended scope practitioner although he was used to working in podiatric surgery and yet he was treading new ground as there was no such pathway laid down within the Royal College of Podiatry Faculties. Each Faculty is concerned with a major part of the overall College's educational workload.

> I had to make my own path as a podiatrist having spent years working in surgery, theatres, giving injections, cannulating, going on advanced lifesaving courses, as well as running a nail surgery list within the hospital supported by anaesthetists. We had a wide range of drugs we could give including intramuscular (IM) and intravascular (IV) as well as prescription only medications. My relationship with trauma and orthopaedics (T&O) grew and I found that the orthopaedic team wanted me to just get on and do it. Perhaps one of my abiding memories came from the fact that a locum consultant orthopaedic surgeon, who I was assisting in theatre with a fractured forearm, asked me my grade. I informed him that I was an ESP and he replied that he thought that I was an orthopaedic consultant. **Damian Holdcroft**

Extended Scope podiatrist in Diabetic Care in the NHS

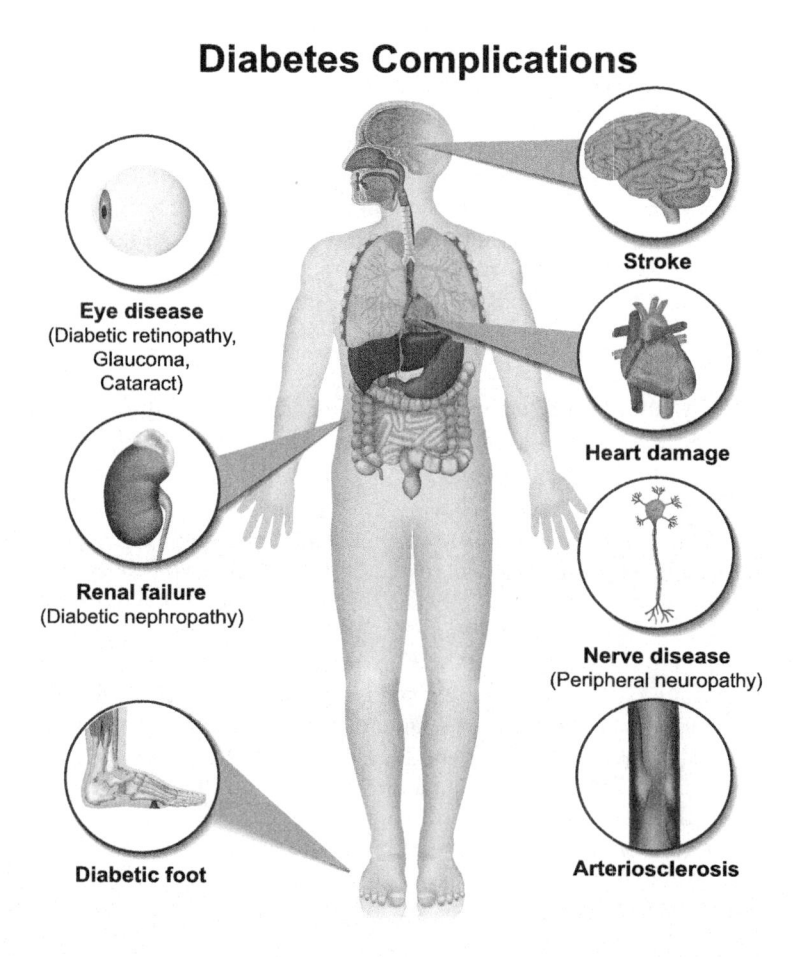

Diabetes Complications

- **Eye disease** (Diabetic retinopathy, Glaucoma, Cataract)
- **Renal failure** (Diabetic nephropathy)
- **Diabetic foot**
- **Stroke**
- **Heart damage**
- **Nerve disease** (Peripheral neuropathy)
- **Arteriosclerosis**

Ian Tarr has been leading the diabetic team in Walsall for over 25 years. He established the unit which is part of a MDT with strong links to the surgeons as well as physicians. Despite the importance of diabetes there is no strict route to becoming an ESP. Ian is on an AfC 8a Grade band.

> I don't think I'm typical because I'm not a manager, I am purely a clinician but I manage my team. Originally I took the surgical route to qualify as a podiatric surgeon. Their multitude of courses helped build my knowledge base. This turned out to be essential for my diabetic work. We took orthopaedics, pharmacology, radiology, and

all those bits were transferable skills into what I do now. It should be designed into modern diabetic training today. I want my team to be able to talk to the medical community at the same (academic) level. It is still for the gratification of the patient. They still need us. There is dependency on us so we're doing something useful like preventing amputations and hopefully providing them with extended lives. Recently we recorded that minor amputations were down from 52-54 to 23 and majors from 18 to 8. Five years ago we were audited and there was a rise in amputations. That caused heads to be raised and that was when we put in for a bid for service funding three and half years ago. Things just evolve in the National Health Service and the only way to get anything to change is just do it! I find you have to worry about the politics afterwards. **Ian Tarr**

Foot protection team

The hospital team comprises 3 people and a foot protection team in the community completes the service. Only one of the three works full-time, while Ian works four days per week.

> It's about preventative medicine and it deals with the whole cardiovascular system for example ABPI, renal function, smoking. You then sign post them to all the relevant agencies. As part of the bid money, we buy and supply footwear. In Walsall, 9% of the population have diabetes. 75% of my patient group are in the lower quarter of income in the UK. Walsall is in a massively deprived area. We would fix the foot then the patients would go out and buy cheap shoes from the local market and then re-ulcerate their foot. We are paying £30 pounds to supply by the national health service. This means they don't need the orthotists' bespoke shoes. This saves masses of money but what's more important is that they wear these shoes whereas historically they don't wear the orthotist's shoes which cost between £400-£500 +each. **Ian Tarr**

The strength of support for diabetes is unquestionable for Ian Tarr and his team and he has managed to find funds for building a new unit where others had failed. He put this down to support; his contacts – as part of building a strong network. Education is very much part of the ESP role and this is rolled out to community GPs

> NHS provision of high-quality care is vital to patients so as to avoid essential services being disinvested. If we are going to be a small service it needs to be high quality with high level of competent staff. A rolling programme provides GPs, practice and district nurses with training in the assessment of the lower limb.

A Career in Podiatric Medicine

> To provide a competency-based programme, socks and shoes come off and they have to demonstrate vascular assessment and neuropathy testing. This is much better now that we have a central point of management and we can see patients within days; when this is delayed it is a problem. We do use PGDs (patient group directives) but rely on medical assistance largely because we work within a MDT and have access to all we need. one of my staff is currently undertaking the I.P course. **Ian Tarr**

Ian writes protocols and has established a foot protection team. He encouraged his colleagues to develop this philosophy as well as take up the Independent Prescribers course. He is a facilitator and works in a densely-packed central hub which works well in this Midlands town.

> We use the national database system, National Diabetes Foot Care Audit (NDFCA), especially around ward work. We encourage ward nurses to screen all the feet coming into the hospital. All the ward work comes from the nurses who find it. They then contact us so we then see the patients. You don't really need many podiatrists in the team. You'll be surprised because we don't do dressings and all that stuff, this is done by GP practices. We are just debriding the patient, offloading, giving them shoes. We're involved with surgeons and decisions to help the diabetic patient, but we keep the clinics small so when the podiatrist is working and the orthopaedic team wants us, we're free and flexible to act for the patients without those lengthy delays. This is done through the fracture clinic. I'm quite passionate as I have done it is so long. **Ian Tarr**

Ian used to teach MSK at the local Birmingham School of Podiatry. His clinical experience makes a difference when teaching brings the real-life experience to the students.

> When a team works together, it's an amazing thing. As my knowledge of wounds grew, I found I could tell which pathogen was caused by the smell they made. I fully understood the impact on someone's life and helping them through an amputation. The change brought about by people's behaviour and the whole psychology appealed to me in huge buckets. **Emily Haworth**

Monitoring Blood Flow

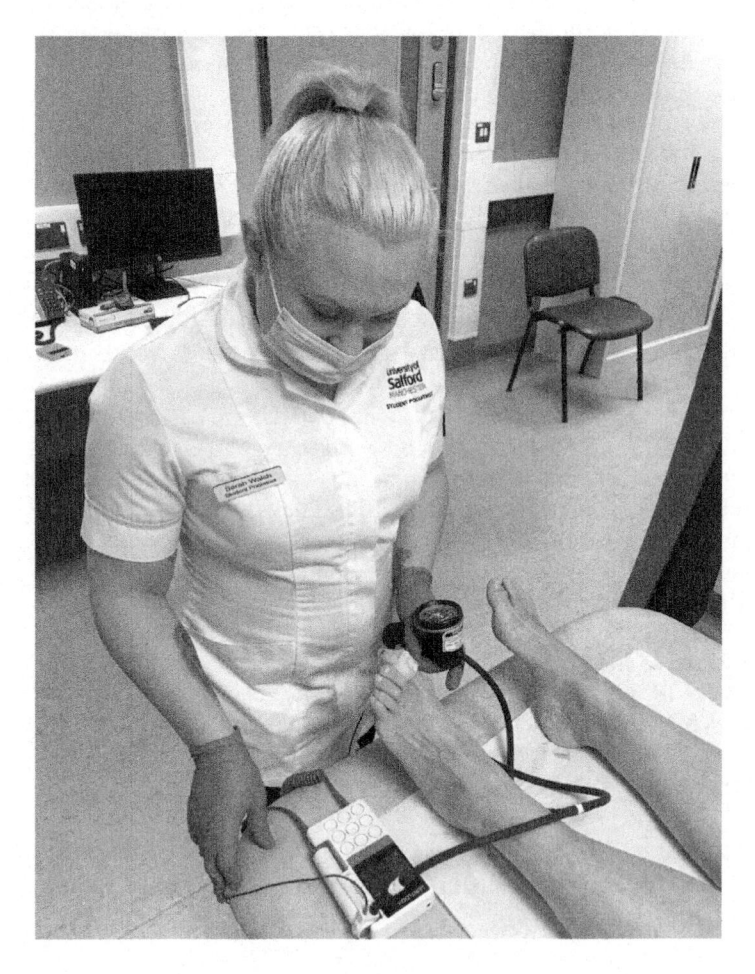

Student Sarah measuring the smallest blood vessels (capillary) pressures in the great toe as part of vascular assessment of the foot in Salford's university clinic. (with permission Sarah Walsh – c/o Martin Fox)

Emily Haworth contrasts different working practices. Emily is also an ESP working within a team led by a consultant physician. 'Lead' means someone who holds the overall budget and takes some managerial responsibility as a clinician. Most podiatrists are experienced at this stage having worked with other senior podiatrists and medics. Nurses are often very well qualified and nurse practitioners with extended scope capabilities may work with the team.

A Career in Podiatric Medicine

Podiatrists pay special attention to patient blood sugars. This means they have to know the correct tests to order to make sure that circulating sugar is not too high. The correct value is 4.0 to 5.4 mmol/L (72 to 99 mg/dL) when fasting but 40 mg/dl or below normally. Wounds not only need to be kept clean but purged of infection. This means that skills with using a scalpel are essential, so any dead tissue is removed and knowledge of the organisms inhabiting wounds is required to work out which antibiotics are sensitive to that strain. Cutting back tissue until healthy bleeding occurs seems quite the opposite of what one might think.

Blood flow, known as vascular status, is checked from the groin to the foot. The many tributaries can become furred up, blocked and reduce the efficiency of supply, more so under exercise. Normal blood flow has the effect of removing waste products and supplying oxygenated nutrients to the skin, muscles and nerves.

Once someone with diabetes is found to be unstable, advice is paramount. Hypoglycaemic events indicate the importance of their blood sugar being regulated by diet and medications used to help improve the pancreas organ where insulin is manufactured. These 'hypos' as they are called demonstrate how the body responds with confusion, irritability and, at worst, sleepiness leading to coma.

Podiatrists have to have an intimate knowledge of pressure measurement under the foot and use this knowledge to offload pressure which causes damage to the foot's skin tissue.

Saving limbs

Emily accepts there are no guarantees in saving limbs and points out that they are seeing patients younger and younger these days. One female died at 32. She saw her before she died. She talked about a 58-year-old active farmer she was treating. The farmer was at risk of a double or bilateral amputation which makes the podiatrist's responsibility tough.

> The infection affected the bones of his right foot. He once cried on my shoulder because of his financial situation. I tried to keep him as mobile as I could but offload the pressure from his foot. The dual conditions add to the challenge. He hopes to self-discharge, but I know within 2-3 weeks, we'll be back to square one again.

On the brighter side, she relates the story of an Aer Lingus pilot who had already lost his left leg when he first came to see her.

> We were struggling to hold onto the right leg. For 2 years, we battled to save this limb. I went over to Switzerland to learn about Appligraf and brought the information back. These are dressings and are only available in the USA. I used the graft on my patient and it worked. The pilot's dream was to ride horses, a passion that I shared. Fifteen months on, he sat proudly on a horse with his new leg. **Emily Haworth**

Emily's stories fit in with her enthusiasm and passion for podiatry at the high-risk end practice.

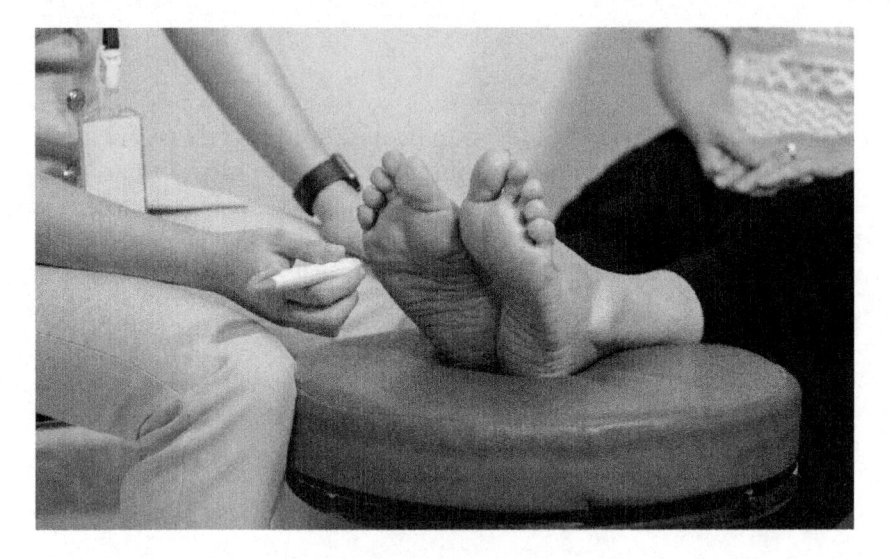

All patients with diabetes will be tested for the ability to feel sensation using fine monofilaments as part of the screening process

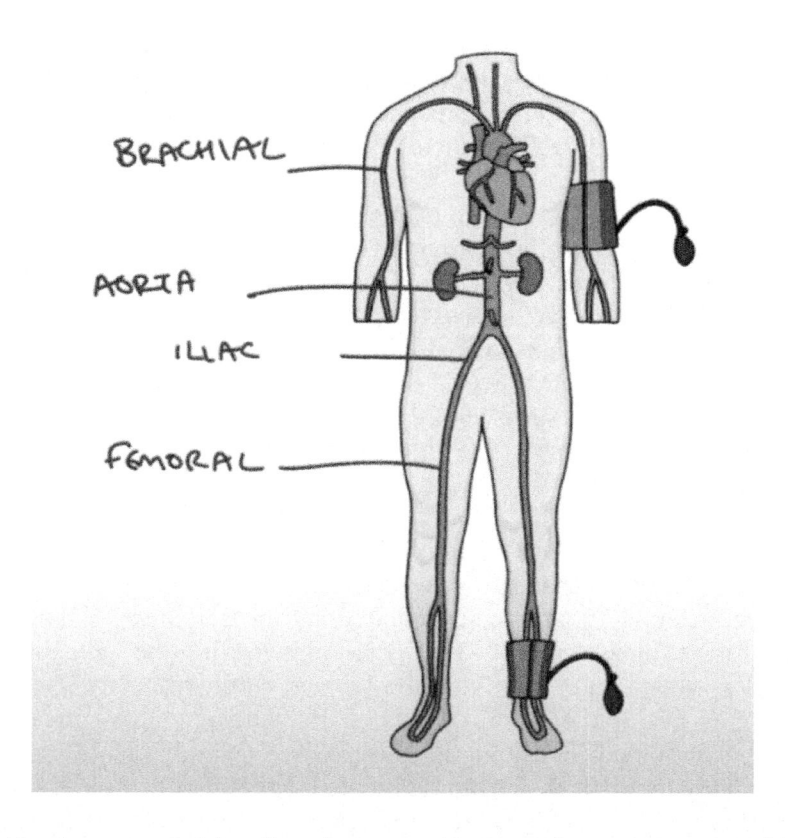

The blood pressure is taken from the arm and leg to make an assessment of the potential blood flow – the measurement is called the ankle-brachial pressure index

The Vascular Practitioner

While Emily and Ian focus on diabetic disease, Martin Fox, returned to the UK from India and started up a new process back in his own geographical area. His story is related to the process he followed in becoming part of a screening team for aortic aneurysm. This is a relatively new concept in podiatry taking on medical diseases at a higher level.

> Supplied with a room, a laptop and mobile phone I designed the community diabetes podiatry job from scratch. **Martin Fox**

Martin believes that as clinicians we should lead on lower limb healthcare narrowing boundaries with other professionals who have historically 'owned' the knee, hip, vascular disease, wound care or dermatology. As podiatry branches out and realises its full potential, he feels we should accept shared responsibility where relevant, elsewhere in the body.

Vascular podiatry is an exciting new specialty, overlapping with the diabetic and high-risk foot, providing early diagnosis and best treatment for life and limb-threatening circulation disease, working in collaboration with hospital vascular teams, set in accessible community clinics. Supporting healthcare provision became even more important during the COVID pandemic, when access to hospital services needed to focus on urgent life and limb-threatening needs. Being knowledgeable in the vascular system is essential with a sound knowledge of the venous and arterial tree.

Following on from Martin's scalpel skills, his knowledge of pulses, and wound care, he expanded into vascular clinical diagnostics. Using handheld Doppler equipment, he undertook measurement of blood flow categorising measurements. His skills allowed him to take on more complex wound care, involving the leg and cardiovascular risks, rather than foot health alone. As the podiatric surgeon takes on a wider assessment of medical health, the musculoskeletal podiatrist examines the upper body and pelvis. Martin had to evaluate pulses behind the knees, into the groin and even in the tummy. This made sense as the blood supply does not start in the foot – it ends there.

> I learned how to feel for an aneurysm on the tummy. The surgeon was saying, if you're seeing these patients, Martin, and they're not coming to me anymore because they're seeing you and you're turning them around to be managed by the GPs for their leg and cardiovascular risks, perhaps you can learn to examine the tummy and palpate the abdominal aorta. If there is an undiagnosed aneurysm sitting under that belly, you too can find it and make sure those patients do come to us. **Martin Fox**

When he found his first large aortic **aneurysm** it was a moment not to be forgotten. If he had missed this vital clue the patient could have died. *"The work really is about lives and limbs,"* he points out. Podiatrists have certainly had to extend their ability and skills contributing to the value of professionalisation toward the health care system.

A Career in Podiatric Medicine

Before long, femoral pulse auscultation (listening with a stethoscope or doppler) led to him being persuaded that if he was to become a vascular practitioner, with a focus on the lower limb, he needed to be doing the other things as well.

Martin has pushed the boundaries of podiatry, to better meet the population's health needs for improved diagnosis and treatment of lower limb arterial disease. This has led him to write journal articles and book chapters, presenting at local, national and international conferences and even presenting on Vascular Podiatry to All Party Parliamentary committees in the Houses of Parliament. Not bad for a young man who once messed up his A levels.

One can practice at different levels but if you really want to specialise in protecting limbs and saving lives, the climate and population need is ever present to make a new contribution with podiatry.

It is no longer unusual to see podiatrists using stethoscopes as this is part of the diagnostic process of monitoring blood pressure as well as other useful sounds. It is likely that we will see more and more advanced practitioners widening their medical assessment (*See Karl Guttormsen*)

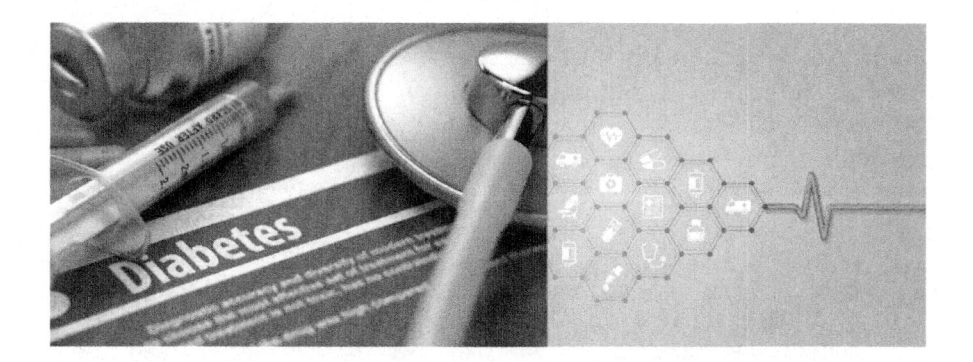

Cancer management

Podiatrists do not actually treat cancer as such. This falls to the oncologist – the cancer specialist, but multidisciplinary teams work together using their own specialist skills to support the framework of care. Afni Shah Hamilton's involvement in cancer care actually started out through her interest in wound care treatment.

> One of my patients was a younger patient under the vascular care at Barnet General. The consultant saw my work in treating a complex ulcer and phoned me to ask if I could treat his patients. The vascular consultant started recommending patients to me, and then word got out more widely in the oncology department through positive feedback from the patients. Other patients who had cancer came to me via word of mouth. **Afni Shah Hamilton**

Being pleased with her exposure and success with these referrals, Afni started to undertake more research on cancer treatment and the adverse effects that cancer medications had on patients. Afni was concentrating on the impact cancer had on the lower limb, either directly or indirectly as a result of their treatment programme. This expertise has steadily developed over the years, including awareness of how different ethnic groups might be impacted differently by certain medications, and now she's helping to share this knowledge with other podiatrists through journal articles in an effort to improve awareness. When she became involved with Macmillan Cancer Support, she was used as an independent podiatrist to sit on the advisory board.

> That was quite a big thing because no one was sitting for them from podiatry. Cancer patients don't typically qualify for podiatric treatment under the NHS, despite all these side effects, and there was no real link into the private sector. **Afni Shah Hamilton**

Afni has now broadened her training to cover wider pain management, using her podiatric and anatomical training to help patients manage more complex and inter-connected pain issues across their whole body. She sees this as a natural extension of her cancer work and is increasingly using these skills to support 'post-cancer' patients who have been managing or living with a variety of pain-related issues during their treatment but now need support in helping their bodies recover some of their former movement.

Diversifying into cancer management is not common amongst podiatrists and her focus on reducing pain and suffering due to many side effects from medications used to treat cancer is unique and unchartered.

> There are so many people facing cancer today who would benefit from treatment and just don't realise what can be done to ease their pain. And in terms of podiatric expertise, cancer's not a scary thing or beyond our capabilities. **Afni Shah Hamilton**

'At-Risk' translates into diabetes for most. Preventing loss of limb versus saving a limb is at the centre of this specialty. However keeping people active should always appeal to reason and common sense from both a medical viewpoint and political point of view based around economy. Poor health with chronic disease is enormously expensive and leads to bed blocking in hospitals. Podiatrists are still under utilised in some aspects of healthcare but multidisciplinary teams are including podiatrists more and more as their value is appreciated.

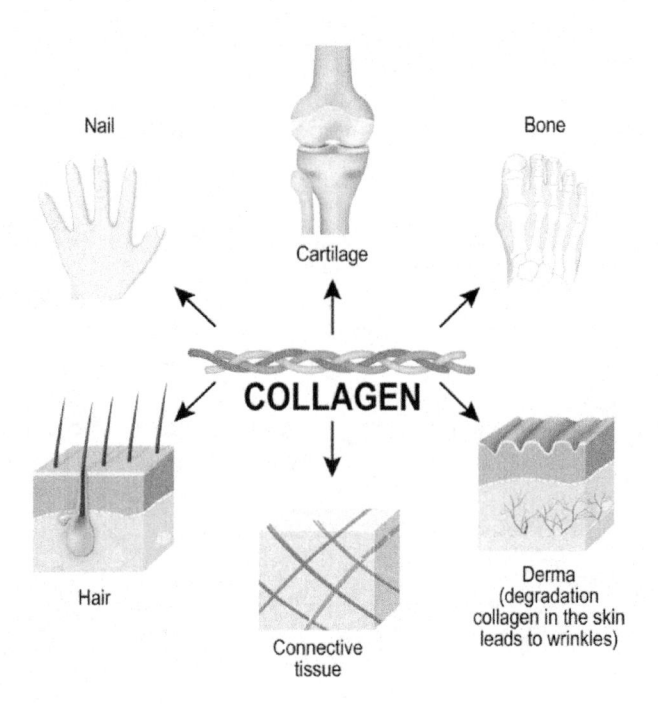

Diagram: COLLAGEN at center with arrows pointing to Nail (hand), Cartilage (knee joint), Bone (foot), Hair (skin with follicles), Connective tissue, and Derma (degradation collagen in the skin leads to wrinkles).

Rheumatology
Extended Scope Podiatrist in Rheumatology

A little behind diabetes comes the arthritic foot focusing initially on rheumatoid disease. The idea of the rheumatoid foot as being distorted and misshapen has changed with modern drugs. Today the question raised by recent research has sought to answer why podiatric contribution rheumatology is not as successful as the publicity around NHS diabetic footcare. If we were to place a single emphasis on rheumatology, we would need to focus on disease and problems with collagen. This tissue affects so many aspects of human movement, from skin to muscles, from cartilage to bone.

Modern podiatry is finding new ways to explore and expand its role once seen as rather more localised than it is today. Rheumatology is an exciting and still developing area in the fields of the NHS, research and even the independent sector. MSK has established plenty of side roots and rheumatology the study of diseases associated with connective tissue, is not only exciting but has plenty of room for career development.

> I have always considered MSK podiatry to be different to rheumatology podiatry. Sadly all too often rheumatology patients with an MSK complaint are put into a generic MSK clinic and there is lack of multidisciplinary communication. Having worked in all areas of podiatry over the years, I can honestly say that working as part of the rheumatology team has been most rewarding. The patients are grateful for the knowledge and understanding of their disease. A lot of patients are in chronic pain with one joint affected or multiple joints and may have tried numerous treatments. They appreciate the help and kindness associated with trying to provide relief of their symptoms. As with all these roles, the ESP in the NHS is a senior clinical role starting at AfC band 7 – although we are currently using the term rheumatology for the specialisation of this field, it is currently underrepresented. **Hayley Edginton** - *Lecturer University of Salford*

> In the case of one patient an elderly lady had a very bad ulceration on the sole of her foot. For four months she'd been coming to our clinic in Ireland, but it wasn't getting any better, mostly because the people who were treating her were thinking of a diabetic foot and they weren't thinking that she had rheumatoid arthritis. and they were just focusing on this. Just offloading, offloading, but they weren't thinking of her medication. It turned out to be supressed healing due to steroids. The ulcer went from four centimetres to fully-healed. Rheumatoid patients seem to heal faster than diabetics. **Christopher Joyce** - *Extended Scope Podiatrist in Rheumatology, Homerton Hospital*

After graduation Chris became involved with a private sports clinic using his MSK skills. He did that for a year, developed skills, made friends, and it's only really when he moved to London, in early 2017 when he started in Homerton, that he noticed there was a gap in service provision for rheumatology patients.

As an AfC Band 5 (graduate), he started to work on rheumatology and shadowed Consultant Podiatric Surgeon, Trevor Prior.

> I went from a Band 5 to Band 6 and then my current Band 7 in rheumatology; there was just a lot of inequalities particularly within the NHS. In terms of podiatry, it's all given to the high risk diabetic foot, nothing to the rheumatoid, even though ulceration rates are still

similar, not amputation rates, or mortality rates. I just really wanted to get rid of the inequality that I saw. That's what's driving me today about it. But in terms of how I've developed my skills and knowledge - I've just done a two-year master's degree in Rheumatology from South Wales University (March 2020). I thought that would solidify all my learning and give me some backup when I want to go and reduce these inequalities in podiatry in terms of the rheumatic foot versus the diabetic foot. I'm very research focused, and I'm very academic. So in my opinion, yes, I think some type of master's degree - it doesn't have to be a full blown master's degree, it can be a post grad certificate or diploma - but I think you need that. I can learn all the rheumatology skills, no problem in terms of podiatry, but to have the medical management, the MDT management, kind of the holistic approach, that's when I wanted to do a Master's. I just wanted to encompass everything that rheumatology is. I didn't want to focus just on rheumatology podiatry. **Christopher Joyce**

The problems with poor healing, diminished blood supply, overloading of forces under the foot lead to ulcers. While diabetes and leprotic patients have variable levels of loss of nerve sensation, many ulcers are due to neglect and a wide variety of problems from blood vessel blockage, aneursyms as well as organ failure. Some ulcers can become malignant.

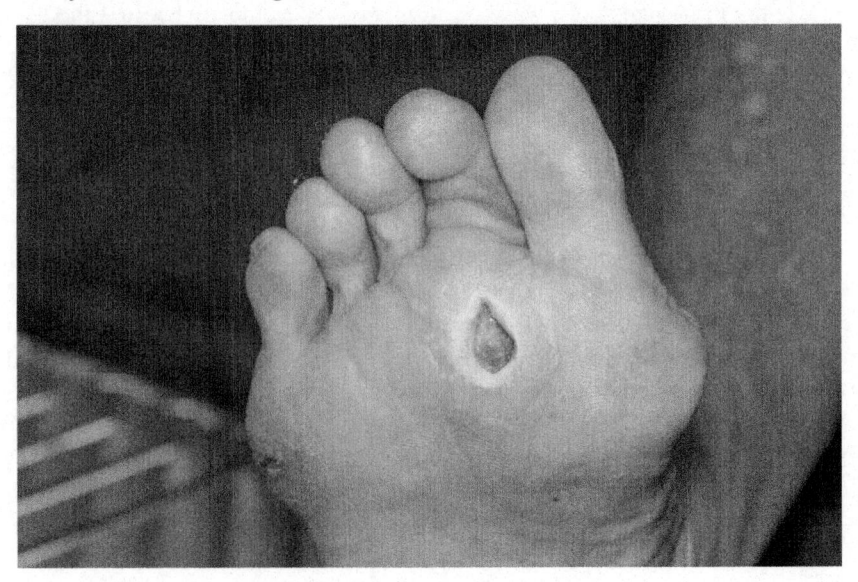

A *trophic ulcer* with callus under the side of the foot shows evidence of abnormal mechanical loads

Podiatry Rheumatic Care Association

Many different special interest groups within podiatry under one roof.

> A number of people started up an association around 1996 called the *Podiatry Rheumatic Care Association*. With the advent of the Royal College of Podiatry conferences bringing together all the different special interest groups within podiatry the Royal College of Podiatry (RCoP) Faculty of Podiatric Medicine became home to all the groups now known as advisory groups and through this advise the RCoP on all aspects of clinical strategy. When it comes to rheumatoid arthritis people talk about multimorbidity these days; a person may not 'just have' rheumatoid arthritis, or they may not 'just have' diabetes. Once upon a time specialising in one aspect or condition was competitive with many charismatic authority leaders influencing evolvement of the profession in this way. Now our skills are recognised as much broader and important to managing foot health across a whole range of diverse and often complex conditions. **Cathy Bowen** – *Lecturer University of Southampton*

Alongside rheumatoid disease Chris looks at other forms of arthritis like psoriatic arthritis and reactive arthritis as well as vasculitis (blood vessel inflammation). On one occasion he diagnosed and started team management of the rarer Behcet syndrome. This is characterised by foot and genital ulcers, fatigue, eye pain and joint pain. With treatment his patient is now able to manage. In his extended role he can use imaging (X-rays and scans) blood tests and it is his close association with the rheumatologist that allows a positive partnership.

Mixing skills
> The use of diagnostic ultrasound by podiatrists has made a difference to diagnosis because you can detect if it's synovitis (joint inflammation) or not. Over the counter footwear is issued and made-to-measure shoes are not used as much as they were one as I don't see any of these major deformities, but custom made orthoses are used.

> The major component of my role is patient education. That is the main focus of what I do when I see my patients because again the rheumatologist doesn't have time to explain. They give them a leaflet but most of the time they won't read it. So, what I do is I talk about their disease to them, how it affects their foot and ankle now, and maybe in the future, and how we can limit that.

So my focus really is on that holistic approach, explaining to them what their disease is, giving them simple exercises, muscle stretches, good footwear advice, but orthoses are my key management. As an ESP I have to focus on the pharmacology, the MSK, the vascular, a lot of other different medical specialties into one, where the nurse really only has to focus on the rheumatology part of it. We are that kind of multi-dimensional physician in a way. **Christopher Joyce**

Sadly though, there aren't many clinical placements on offer to support this teaching and so students have less exposure to patients in this field. **Hayley Edginton**

When you're at university there is the opportunity to undertake the high risk work, the kind of debridement, that type of wound work, everyday care, which tends to take some people down the path of diabetes, and then there's the musculoskeletal, the biomechanics - that side, which tends to go towards the sports injuries or the musculoskeletal field. **Heidi Siddle** - *Consultant Podiatrist, Leeds Teaching Hospitals NHS Trust*

Dr Heidi Siddle works closely with medical teams. She was able to combine different skills from several fields adding to her contribution to Rheumatology. When you add a research element the umbrella of opportunity widens.

I could look after the people who have got the weird and wonderful connective tissue diseases that present with open wounds, that present with fragile skin, that are high risk, they have vascular complications, unusual vascular complications. That's exacerbated by musculoskeletal problems, and the musculoskeletal problems are not because somebody wants to get back to running the 100 metres as fast as they can do. These are people who want to be able to carry out everyday activities where their feet have been affected by their underlying disease. They've got pain, they're not like our diabetics where they lose sensation, lose feeling. It's a whole different entity. But these are people who just want to be able to walk around, you know, everyday life. **Heidi Siddle**

How do postgraduates climb the ladder within rheumatology?
Progression in rheumatology, appears to differ from Trust to Trust. In my experience, I did postgraduate studies to support my learning, whilst at the same time, making a proposal *('selling myself')* to the rheumatology team within the outpatient department as to what I could offer their service and how my treatment would differ to that of a 'normal' podiatrist. This took some convincing with the old school consultants but new age consultants with experience of

A Career in Podiatric Medicine

working with AHP's saw the benefit of multi-disciplinary working with specialist AHP's. The clinic developed by trialling one session a week which later resulted in a six-month waiting list, a business case for more sessions and eventually a full-time position working as an Advanced Podiatrist in Rheumatology. **Hayley Edginton**

In general terms this area of specialty is underdeveloped. As with podiatric surgery, forensics and even dermatology, new branches emerge only when clinicians themselves push the boundaries of the existing podiatry landscape.

The clinical landscape will always grow where professionals develop themselves rather than expect the scope of a certain practice to expand by magic.

For the student at school or even undergraduate, an emphasis should be placed on being prepared to think outside the box and reach for the sky – there is no limit to where podiatry can continue to reach.

High-Risk Podiatry

By the time the reader has reached this part of the book the word high-risk will have been used repeatedly. The term diabetes and ulcer will have dominated many sentences and descriptions. To make it perfectly clear, it is important to appreciate that anyone practising podiatry is trained to deal with the high-risk foot whether they be a specialist or a generalist, whether it be in clinic or on a house visit. These are standards which come under essential duties.

What does high-risk mean?

I suspect if you asked most podiatrists what high risk means they would point to an impoverished blood supply. While this would be correct mostly – it is not quite true in all respects. A limb is also at risk from skin disease, infection, deteriorating nerve supply, chronic pain, cancer and from injury. Therefore we can say all podiatrists can make a judgement on each condition but perhaps they may not have the scope to manage all conditions. The conditions illustrated in **Table 2** illustrate the point that high risk arises from a range of conditions not just one - diabetes. I should point out this list is not exhaustive and serves as an example of conditions taught in medicine and pathology. In each case the foot can swell, ulcerate or start to become necrotic (death of tissue).

Infection can spread rapidly and death can follow from heart failure follows with overwhelming infection.

> Epidermolysis bullosa
> Cellulitis
> Peroneal nerve injury
> Popliteal aneurysm
> Occlusive angio-thrombosis obliterans
> Trench foot
> Sensory-motor neuropathy
> Complex regional pain syndrome
> Compartment syndrome
> Osteosarcoma
> Diabetes mellitis
> Necrotizing fasciitis
> Tendon rupture tibialis posterior

Table 2 shows a range of high risk conditions

This list shown above highlights some complex medical conditions (see glossary) affecting the foot. Treatment can only be based on accurate diagnosis using modern diagnostic tools. Medication needs to be tailored to the condition and in some cases surgery is necessary. It would be misleading to suggest podiatrists perform treatment in all cases although those qualified in foot surgery can manage most conditions as long as the patient's health has not deteriorated so that they require medical stabilisation.

> An 80-year old working farmer came to my clinic one day following failure in his toe to heal for months - an ultrasound image showed he had a popliteal aneurysm (at knee level). Although rare, the ballooning of the artery starved his foot of oxygen. Intervention prevented his leg from being amputated. With podiatry having reliable diagnostic techniques we can offer better screening. **David Tollafield**

Multidisciplinary teams (MDTs) are formed from a number of specialist groups including medical physicians, consultant surgeons (plastic, vascular, general and orthopaedic), orthotists, physiotherapists, pain specialists as well as podiatrists. In some cases there will be a need to bring in neurologists, oncologists, rheumatologists and gastroenterologists.

What makes a specialist in high-risk

Clearly the main branch of high-risk limb preservation falls to those with the most common disease – diabetes. Type 2 occurs later in life and patients live with the changes which may not always appear quickly. Healing wounds can take months.

Uncontrolled diabetes eads to amputations, often affecting the leg below the knee. Following amputations a patient's life is shorter - diabetes is a killer. It consumes millions of pounds in care, surgery, hospitalisation, prosthetics and drugs. Good education and podiatric monitoring have been found to save limbs and lives.

It does not take a genius to realise now why podiatrists specialise in diabetes care. Podiatrists can change lives and feet really matter. Remove mobility and a patient loses motivation, cannot achieve as much as if he or she has both legs, becomes obese faster and joints deteriorate, as do muscles.

Podiatry is respected as part of the MDT and money follows such services along with cancer and heart disease. High-risk diabetic care is a good career to follow and reaches AfC Band 8 with specialist or consultant status. It is worth joining some experienced podiatrists who have made this their career goal.

Life changing events - early days
>One day I saw a lady who had a wound that just would not heal. This particular wound went through her foot. We tried everything from syringing with saline and washing it out and packing with different products on the market. And then the district nurse called in a little early one day and found that the lady was sitting in her lounge with a knitting needle through her foot, exciting out of her sole. And when she asked her about it, *"what are you doing?"* The lady was most embarrassed; she'd been caught out. It transpired that she was so terribly lonely that she was using this knitting needle to keep the wound open because if she kept the wound open, and the wound didn't heal, she could keep coming back in to see me. **Suzy Taylor**

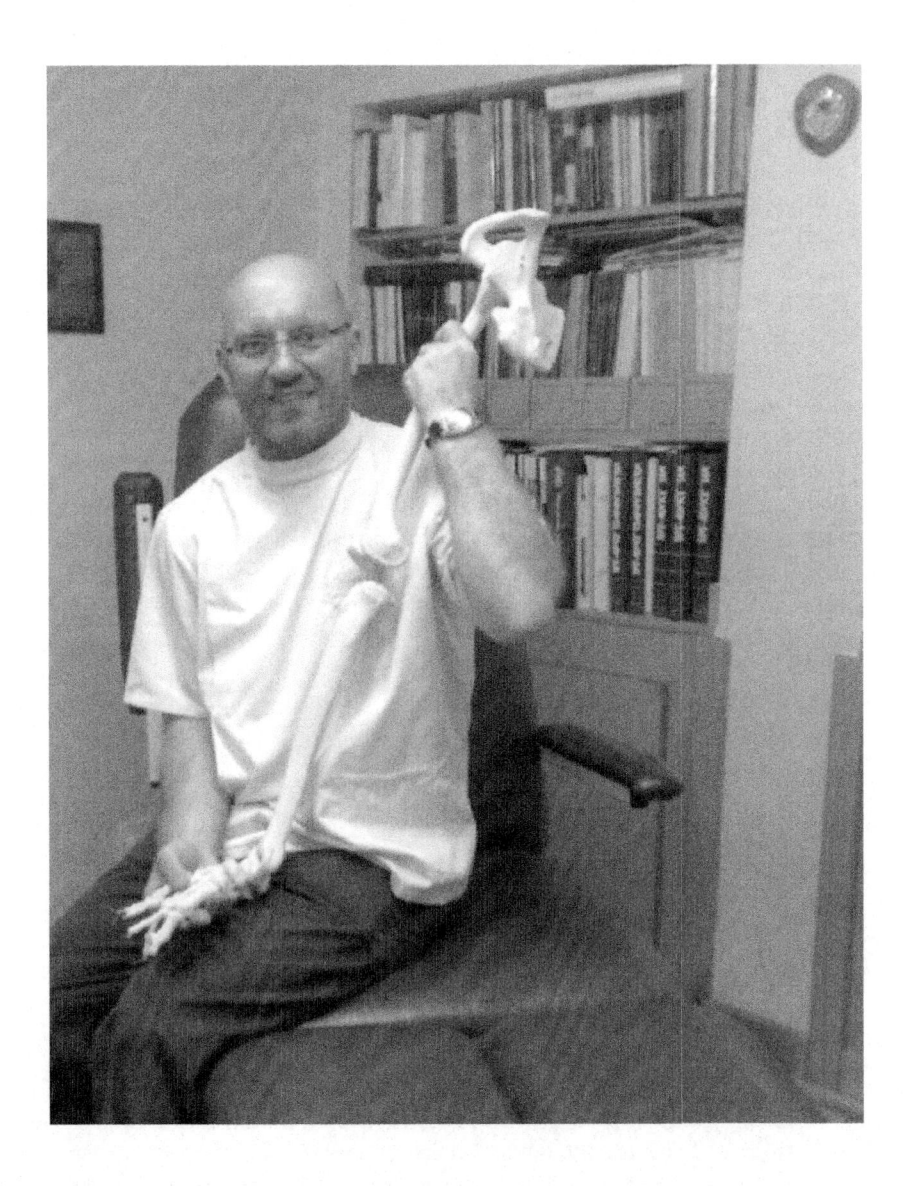

Jonathan Small in clinical practice with a full set of lower limb bones (plastic) with half pelvis

Musculoskeletal Podiatry

Core podiatry has been coined as a phrase covering skin, nail management, footwear and health education. Since Dr Lisa Farndon published her seminal work on private and NHS practice – MSK work has proven to be a core part of podiatry. Harmonising MSK with the skin surface has never been more important and the subject simply migrates into other subjects such as diabetes, tissue damage at all levels and of course podiatric surgery. MSK is no less important when it comes to ensuring our patients are mobile. There are a number of connective tissue diseases that fall under the medical banner of rheumatology. This specialisation is dealt with separately.

Few general podiatry practitioners fail to understand how critical MSK work is within their practice, be it NHS or the independent sector. Google your local podiatry service and it is almost certain that the word orthoses-biomechanics-sports-musculoskeletal will appear somewhere on the website landing page.

MSK in podiatry can be taken as far as the clinician wishes and it mixes in with our NHS and independent practice careers. MSK can also integrate with Podiatric Sports Medicine

Combining industry

The idea of becoming engaged with the industrial side of healthcare appealling.

> We can measure pressure, but not shear forces clinically. Lenny was a boxer and kept getting blisters on his lead foot. This was the one he was pushing off with his right big toe. No matter what he tried, that blister would cause havoc. He tried a few of the usual things - Compeed plasters and double socks and the whole gambit and things. Not being beaten, Lenny came up with an insole, a shop-bought insole template, and his blister incidents stopped. He knew he was onto something. By creating a three-dimensional image on a screen, you can prescribe anything, add anything, and remove anything. It has an intuitive way of working. We thought the original machine was from Star Trek; it was able to mill out a complete insole in seven minutes, and it required minimal post-production grinding and cleaning up. Perhaps it needed a cover. This new machine will mill

four sets of insoles in 50 minutes or less. **Mike McColgan** - *Independent Podiatrist*

Because Mike was working on the diabetes side of podiatry, he was involved with a computer system (CAD-CAM) and set out to reduce diabetic foot complications and the high amputation rate. The people he was working with hoped that they could take the idea into a new arena. And this is how he became involved with Pellitec Ltd.

Reducing surgical intervention

The vast majority of foot and ankle MSK work is 80% conservative and 20% surgery, in round about terms. So, a lot of the orthopaedic surgeon's time was being spent not doing foot & ankle surgery. At that time they were looking for someone to come in and do more of the conservative care, and if it wasn't for a GP being a bit grumpy and not taking the post up, I wouldn't have been offered it. I was only invited to go along because I wasn't a surgeon. **Jai Saxelby** – *Independent Podiatrist*

Having moved to Sheffield, Jai became involved with the running shops called *Gait Analysis Shoe Prescription (GASP)* - at Sheffield University. Developing his network of contacts led him to a couple of orthopaedic surgeons who had high reputations in the field of MSK work. Jai found his progress slower at one point until the orthopaedic team at Sheffield were looking for 'the non-surgical stuff,' as he puts it. His work with orthopaedics has allowed him to reduce the number of patients going to surgery. Jai's approach has benefitted patients as podiatry now sees anything foot and ankle as well as higher up the skeletal frame.

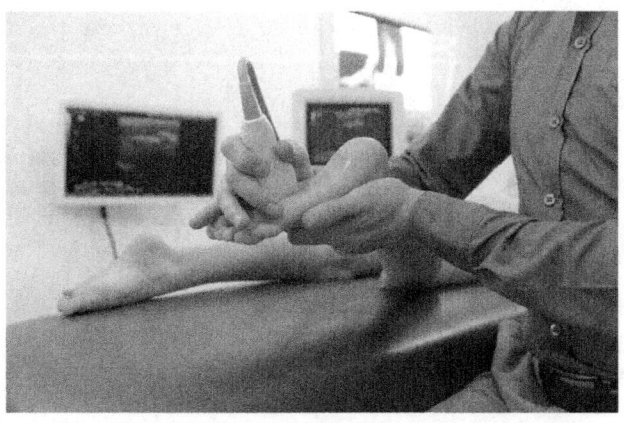

Ultrasound has become a very important new development in assessing conditions of the foot, ankle and lower limb for the MSK specialist

Prison Work

Jonathan Small, is a generalist and an independent podiatrist and business mentor. He started working for two prisons, of which one was a maximum-secrity prison. The departure into this unusual area came about as a result of his work with diabetes where he had engaged in some group talks. One of the GPs happened to work in the prison service. Jonathan appreciated that developing a comprehensive footservice in house was essential within the prison service. The type of problems seen in prison were not so different to those Jonathan saw in the community.

In a maximum-security prison, the big challenge was working with a sharp instrument, a scalpel, within a maximum-security prison in a room on your own.

> You had a really heightened awareness of everything. You didn't go in there all lackadaisical about it. You knew that potentially the wrong prisoner on the wrong day with the wrong mindset, and you're at risk. So yes, we developed some really good skills in awareness and patient handling. **Jonathan Small** – *Independent Podiatrist*

Working with Branded Companies

After leaving the NHS, Claire Carr joined Scholl - now a well-known brand name. Scholl had shops on most town high streets, and this provided a different brand of footcare but in a commercial setting. After six months, she left to join Boots. Claire found that Boots were teaching transferable skills - lessons she was able to bring to her private practice. She then secured a job with Shuropody, a company who took over from Scholl.

> I went to work with them, but I worked with them in their head office so it wasn't really a clinical role. It was more of a kind of managerial role, and it was looking at different aspects of recruitment, clinical supervision, standard setting, and passing knowledge about how we discuss what someone needs and what we give to them without being salespeople, but being healthcare professionals. With Boots, I'd also undergone some management training. I'd been involved in some of their training in terms of the biomechanics in order to try and get everybody up to a standard. So there was still a bit of a clinical hands-on but ended up doing more of a management role. **Claire Carr**

While Claire had different types of jobs within podiatry over a span of 32 years her own expertise led her to work with another podiatrist orientated around custom orthotic manufacturer. She decided to investigate different orthotic suppliers and met a few, and one of the people was the CEO of Firefly Orthotics. He asked Claire to work for him. She fitted her industrial work into the working week, attending stands at the National Conference, Sports Medicine conferences as well as paediatrics conferences.

Football and Orthoses

Trevor Prior started to work with a new company producing orthoses in the UK through Canonbury; a podiatry-based distributor. Phil Vasyli had an orthotics lab in Australia called the Vasyli Orthotics Laboratory. Trevor started to undertake lectures in biomechanics on behalf of Vasyli. His work in the field of football expanded at West Ham and involved the training centre at St George's Park in the West Midlands. Of course, employment with the clubs was only part of his work commitment. Over the years, Trevor developed a business approach to his sports activities while maintaining a modest surgery practice. In truth, most podiatrists specialise in one area, but not Trevor. Having travelled out to the USA he started to make contacts, especially in the area of diabetes.

A modern pair of Vasyli ¾ length orthoses with a forefoot wedge (red)

Footwear and research

Another niche area in podiatry

> My clinical experience drives my research interest. Nike were the leaders in developing a shoe to improve energy efficiency and performance of marathon runners. Other companies were not far behind in adopting this shoe styling. **Helen Branthwaite** – *Independent podiatrist, lecturer and researcher*

Helen became interested in footwear early in her career. She provided an input into biomechanics-MSK for her outpatient department in the acute hospital working in tandem with a local podiatric surgeon. Undertaking a MSc degree studying the effect of wedging, she used 3D analysis at the well-equipped Staffordshire University.

Helen has a strong belief that podiatric medical training requires a good understanding of the shoe and its classic anatomy. She is currently researching a new tool for the clinical assessment of footwear. Selecting the correct footwear for the right task is a common flaw for many people, adding to the potential for footwear related problems.

Helen focuses on applying biomechanical principles to understand her patients injuries. She then devises a treatment plan that will alter the load associated with forces affecting their body.

Orthoses, footwear design, strengthening and other modalities allow her patients to recover. Helen's caseload involves triathletes, fell and marathon runners, cyclists and keen hill walkers, all of which fit injury and a high prevalence of foot problems. When one man approached her with his high arched foot (pes cavus), a foot shape known for creating impact problems, he followed Helen to different clinical practices to continue his care.

> The man spent the winter out in Val d'Isere skiing, and he did ridiculous things like being dropped from helicopters and jumping down slopes. Being passionate, he didn't want to give that up. **Helen Branthwaite**

The surgeon told him with some reluctance that he could try a podiatrist but added that he didn't think he would get on very well. This led to a healthy professional relationship between the orthopaedic surgeon and Helen. The patient, now 78, is still doing extreme skiing!

Pic 'n Mix

After graduation it is possible to mix employment between the NHS or the independent sector using part-time contracts or job share opportunities where available. This might suit someone to find that niche. Locum options are also a good way forward.

Locum Work

A locum appointment is usually temporary. You register with one of the many UK companies, and there are a large variety to choose from covering the whole of the UK. As of June 2022 - rates ranged from £17-£30 per hour and permanent placements from £26,000 to £48,000. These figures will change with time but offers the reader some perspective on remuneration.

Companies come and go all the time and looking for those with longer established years of business makes sense. Locum work is popular for initial placement but you will need transport unless you are living in a large city like London. Salaries are at the upper end of the scale for London because of the higher cost of living and are reflected in locum rates. Locum work uses NHS AfC bands of which Band 6-7 is most common but Band AfC 5 does crop up. It is possible for new graduates to pick up a Band AfC 6, but don't expect it.

> At the time of qualifying there were a couple of agencies that I was registered with. Quite often I would get a call in the morning – *"We need you to cover a clinic because someone's ill."*
>
> If you're the type of personality who enjoys variety and not having a fixed location, or even knowing where you might work day to day, this might appeal. You could find it stressful just having to walk into unknown situations so you need to be quite adaptable. I think you gain incredible experience in doing that because you see how different departments work. **Louise Kennedy**

Using a scooter Louise whizzed across London to do a day in an NHS clinic here and there and ended up working in nearly every health authority in Greater London. At the time she found she could earn more in a couple of days a week doing locum work than her friends and colleagues working full-time in the NHS.

Independent Practice *v* Employment

Becoming a private practitioner is popular. If you own or set up a private podiatry practice you will most likely become a Sole Trader – no pun intended. Later we will see how some podiatrists become private business managers growing their practice by employing assistant podiatrists or creating partnerships. In some cases the practice will become a Limited (Ltd) Company. The discussion around accountancy and tax efficiency is outside the range of this career book. Try to understand Limited versus Sole Trader/Self-employed versus partnership if you start up your own practice – but take professional advice from an accountant.

Graduates new to employment must decide whether they want more control or prefer the comfort of being employed. Self-employment is where you earn your money and have to declare income and pay tax each year. Employed practice means tax is taken off your monthly pay-as-you-earn (PAYE).

Employed work provides paid holidays, sick pay, pensions and paid courses. Self-employed have to cover their own holidays, sick pay, pensions and pay for their own courses. At present the market is open to podiatrists to develop and compete with other healthcare outlets. Everyone has their own idea where they want to work, but there is no recommended single model.

The dentist with whom Afni had worked as a dental nurse, before she took up podiatry, supported her in launching her own business and allowed her to start seeing private patients at his clinic. Working evenings and weekends, whenever she could fit in the appointments around her NHS day job and the hours of the dental practice. She slowly started to build up a base of regular patient caseload.

Associate Podiatrist
> When you're going into private practice there are many different avenues of employment. With commercial practice (Shuropody for example) you're employed. You can sign up to a locum agency and just work when you wanted too. You can become a Sole Trader, as a smaller business or you can be an associate as well, which is what I do in a couple of practices. The associateship works for me. It's somebody else's practice, they own it, they set it up, and I get a percentage fee for the work that I do on that day. **Claire Carr**

New models of advancement in health care

New models for podiatry professionals are attracting interest. Two professional positions come under development from Health Education England (HEE); First Contact Practitioner and Advanced Clinical Practitioner. The reader is directed to the HEE site – where more information is available:

https://www.hee.nhs.uk/our-work/allied-health-professions/enable-workforce/ahp-roadmaps/first-contact-practitioners-advanced-practitioners-roadmaps-practice

First Contact Practitioner (FCP)

An FCP is a diagnostic clinician working in Primary Care at the top of their clinical scope of practice at Master's level, on AfC Band 7 with reference to lower limb conditions. With additional training, FCPs can build towards advanced practice. The clinician must have a minimum of three years of postgraduate experience in their professional specialty area of practice before starting Primary Care training to become an FCP.

Advanced Clinical Practitioner (ACP)

An ACP is a clinician working at an advanced level across four pillars which involves research, leadership and management, education, and clinical practice. Again this is at master's degree level and remunerated at AfC Band 8a. An AP in Primary Care can develop from a range of specialties, not just podiatry.

We're trailblazers of our day
>Advanced clinical practice means we work at a similar level to our medical colleagues, but we bring with us far more than a junior doctor would. We bring our years of experience in our primary field. I support the junior doctors and of course work with consultant medics. My Master's degree was grounded in a foundational level of medicine. We performed advanced clinical examination skills which includes respiratory exams, genito-urinary and cardiovascular to name some of the systems – *see systems of the body*.

This will include taking 'bloods.' We check markers to show inflammation of the liver and kidney function, which plays an important role in prescribing medicines - such as antibiotics. I work outside of the lower limb and I think I was the first one in the country to go into a role that wasn't linked with the lower limb. There are now seven or eight of us in the country working at this level, or training at this level. We are expected to undertake independent prescribing as part of the MSc or if already attained, another level 7 module; in my case I undertook Acute Medicine as I was an existing I.P. **Karl Guttormsen**

HUMAN BODY SYSTEMS

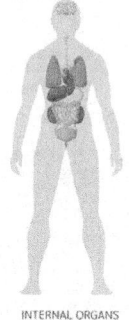

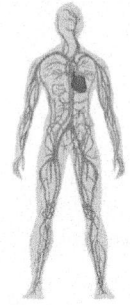

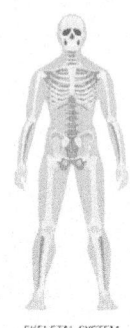

INTERNAL ORGANS   CIRCULATORY SYSTEM   MUSCULAR SYSTEM   SKELETAL SYSTEM

Karl mentions 'systems' of the body which is medical speak for the key working organs and connections of the human body. They are traditionally broken down as follows. Clinically you cannot study one system alone to gain an accurate picture of health.

- Cardiovascular (includes the heart)
- Respiratory (includes the lung)
- Alimentary (includes the liver)
- Genito-urinary (includes the kidney)
- Central nervous system (includes the brain and cranial nerves)
- Locomotor system (includes all joints)
- Endocrine system (includes organs such as thyroid and pancreas)
- Skin

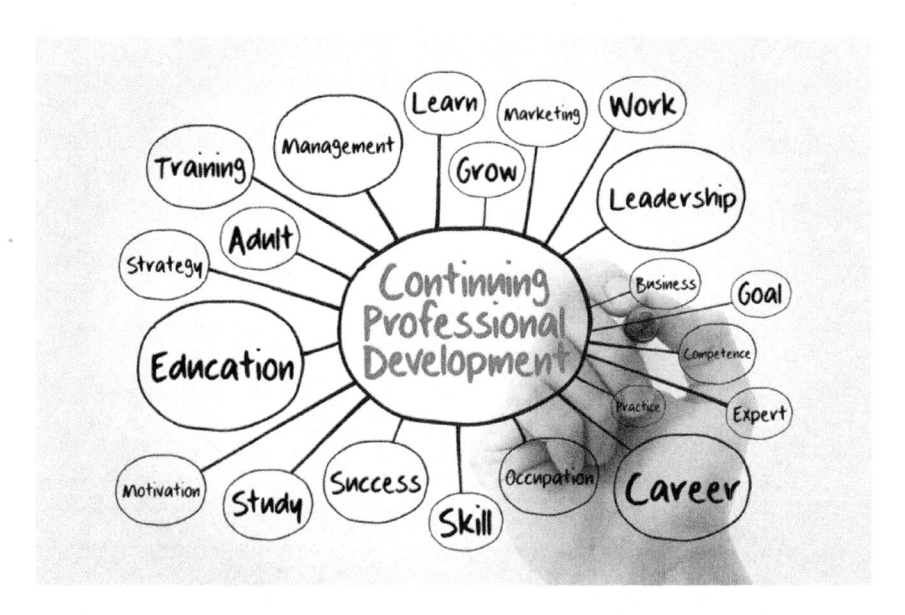

At this point you may think I have covered all the possible options in podiatry.

Leaving graduate school does not immediately lead to your ultimate goal and we use continuing professional development to build our career.

Section 5 provides an overview of further sub-specialisations:

Independent sector
Managers and clinical leads in the NHS
Podiatric sports medicine
Expert witness work
Forensic podiatry
Research
Podiatric surgery

Modern innovation

Author in clinic (2016). Modern systems now use portal digital pictures (PACS) for x-rays. This allows faster viewing for the clinician who can show patients the results immediately. Above and behind the computer screen an older mounted view box is shown (now removed). Prior to the PACS system films were carried in large envelopes and placed on viewing boxes. Computers allow for improved storage, digital enhancement and overlaying with measuring options. The films on view are those of magnetic resonance imaging (MRI) and non radiation form of diagnostic aid.

5- The Developing Profession of Podiatry

Cast your mind back to the start of this career guide and recall the list guiding your preferences as to what to look for in a career guiding your early decision making. Three elements come into business as a healthcare professional.

- An ability to challenge yourself
- Look for new opportunities beyond the original career
- Consider the importance of financial reward & security

We can gain some insight from podiatrists working in different sectors. There is a new breed of podiatrists who are driven by strong managerial awareness as clinicians. Today there is plenty of advice whereas once such advice was restrictive.

> I stumbled from different practice set ups with little advice armed with only a thin book as a student that said, "Get a bank manager, an accountant and a solicitor!" Even advertising was a problem in those days, limited to six newspaper ads with restrictive narratives. These were the days before websites came along. I mention websites as you

can learn a good deal about podiatry practices from viewing each site. **David Tollafield**

Business mission  | Vision statement  | Competitive intelligence

The Business End of Podiatry

Going into business involves innovation, independence, risk, working alone or working with a team, taking courses in leadership and business, dealing with accountancy, expenditure, aspects of the law, health and safety and, above all, the satisfaction of building your own clinic. These elements create the typical picture that a manager has to deal with. Not everyone wants this responsibility. If you want to go home at night, shut the door and forget about work, then private practice is not for you.

> It is pretty difficult to open a podiatry practice and not survive because the income is relatively strong compared to many other businesses. However, it is easy to lose income by making bad decisions from performing badly. There are so many foot problems out there that most practices, if they are in the right location, and open for the right number of hours, and have an appropriate price point, they will survive. **Tony Gavin** - *Independent Podiatrist & Manager Director OSGO. From Selling Foot Health as Podiatry p22-24 Amazon Books*

Tony explored this side of the business having made mistakes as a younger person in different ventures before entering podiatry as a mature student. He now runs a successful support service for UK based clinical practises offering competion alonsgide the two main professional groups.

Once she had sufficient experience, Debbie Delves (centre) modernised her practice, having bought into an old business (established in 1948). She now has a number of podiatrists working for her

Developing a Modern Practice

Experienced practitioners express the qualities seen in a successful business-led podiatry practice. We often think of a career in management as resting within the NHS. Today management has expanded formally into all areas bringing new opportunities.

> When I first took over in Dulwich, we were engaged in routine practice, the type of activity that podiatry was once described, as such as people couldn't cut their toenails and wanted a bit of hard skin taken off. What we do now is a lot more advanced, and we're forever trying to evolve and make sure that what we're doing is working at the top of our game. We're actually dealing with the cause of the symptoms rather than just the symptoms alone. **Debbie Delves**

Debbie's Dulwich practice was established in 1948. When asked what the difference between working in the independent sector and the NHS – "You'll earn more money," she replied.

> That's an important thing, and that, I think, for the youngsters is actually quite a big driver. You have the potential to earn quite a lot of money in private practice if you do it right. And I do think that's a driver, and I don't think we should be embarrassed about that. **Debbie Delves**

While the modern-day view may become polarised toward advanced techniques, Debbie is aware that the NHS has changed, and the type of roles today have partly become more focused on musculoskeletal services triaging patients to other consultants. She is also aware of the role that podiatric surgery plays. After all, she holds a Master's degree in Podiatric Surgery.

Many people have good technical skills, and while they understand the technicalities of their profession it does not translate into running a business. Debbie is keen to point out after years of running a business that it is a full-time job and she no longer has time for clinical work.

Leadership qualities
> I've got a young team who are really into IT and know what they're doing. And I can say, "Let's have a couple of hours a month where you work on helping me with the blog," for example, I can have them doing all sorts of things that helps the business. It isn't just about a conveyor belt of patients. **Debbie Delves**

Debbie has three podiatrists at the moment working in her practice, with one specialising in MSK, while another one has a special interest in dermatology. She believes that allowing her team to develop is really liberating.

Growing your business
> There is a lot of management time involved in running a private practice with ever-increasing costs. Examples include regulation, maintaining appropriate health and safety protocols, data security and insurance, but perhaps more significantly the way we now operate has changed. It used to just be 'phone calls to arrange appointments, adverts in the local paper, paper patient records and cash payments. Additional costs include website design and maintenance, running payroll and providing pensions for employees, online booking systems, and credit card machines. It is easy to overlook many of these initial steps when developing a private practice as a viable business model. Getting sucked into a lot of start-up expense without fully appreciating the number of patients they'll need to treat before it becomes profitable is something to avoid. **Afni Shah-Hamilton**

Using her former IT skills with MSK work
> IT skills have helped me a huge amount. What it did initially was give me the opportunity to have everything online; everything accessible. People could find the business; they knew what we did

and what we were about. From a financial point of view because I could do all this myself, it meant that there were no extra costs. Every Christmas you'll find me redoing my website as a Christmas treat to myself. I love IT and I love tech. So even from day one, we had an online patient system. In a previous job I used to write hospital systems, so I was very aware of what was required. And I'm very old school, if you don't put the information in, you're not going to get it out. I love data! **Victoria North**

Employment in the private sector

A lot of private practices now will employ people. This seems to be the new emerging way and they're offering some really good supporting packages in terms of pensions and holidays, professional development and continuing education. With their employees, they're trying to make the role as varied as possible. Some of the packages now are fantastic. So it's great as a graduate to actually go out into an employed role and have a team of people around you who can perhaps give you some advice and some guidance. Working with people means less isolation which was typical in the past. **Claire Carr**

Modern treatment technology in practices

Gait analysis
Successful MSK podiatrists need to engage with gait laboratories. One way of expanding is to provide high tech support. As one of Victoria's drives to enlarge her practice, she needed space to house fixed video cameras. The gait laboratory is an extra tool and attracts a large number of runners to her clinic. This is an area she and her business partner are interested in. This means she can help people improve following injuries. She points out that MSK knowledge is essential when evaluating reports to work out what's going on.

Microwave treatment
Victoria recalls a woman in her 20's with a viral skin problem. Her patient was very nervous and her foot had been left without any attention for over six years. Using the latest microwave treatment, which is one of the destructive heat therapies, she destroyed the virus. After the course of treatment Victoria had a fabulous review on her website saying how the patient had been so nervous and yet had giggled through the whole process even though she was scared.

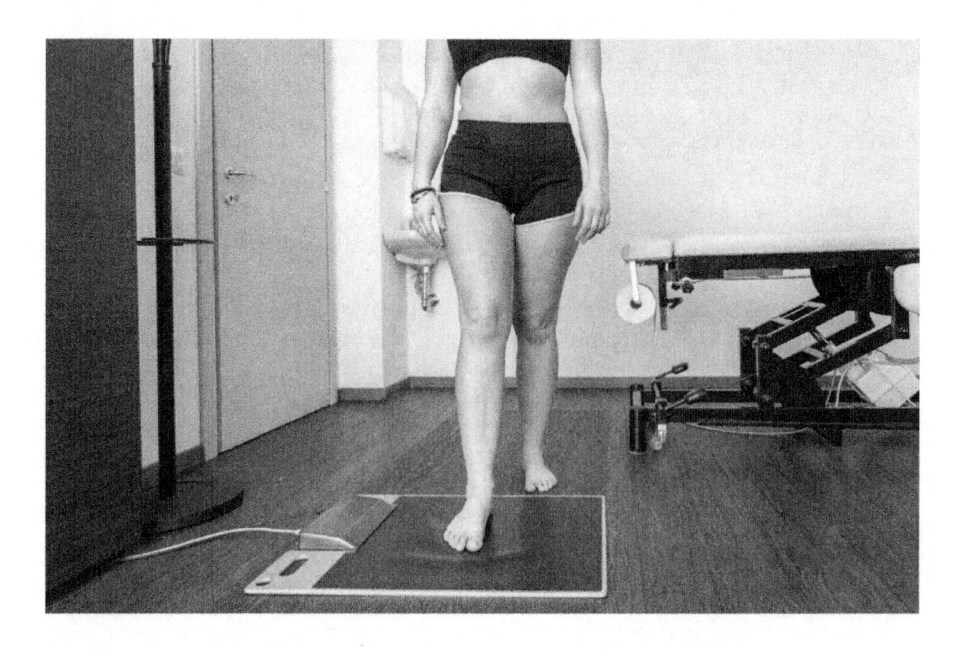

Gait Analysis

All podiatrists have to learn about the science of human movement which is often defined around a walking cycle. While the foot contact is important and can be measured in terms of pressure (see diagram – pressure sensor), the lower limb, pelvis and spine are vital to smooth movement.

The subject is asked to arrive or change into clothing allowing the key parts of the skeleton to be observed. Video cameras and treadmills are also used in gait analysis as the image can be slowed and examined closely. Movement involves rotation and angular changes within the limbs in three dimensions (3D) and can prove difficult to capture with the human eye for small variations.

Muscle conductivity is sometimes added to gait analysis. Modern technology is changing rapidly and once could only be afforded by science establishments. Today equipment has become more cost affordable and used in many clinics. As computers have reduced in size and have greater power, analysis is fast and plays a part in a patient's management plan.

Management in the NHS

Clinical leaders and departmental managers

Changes in the NHS have seen different managerial leads arising from other health disciplines. This might include nurses, physiotherapists or speech therapists as managers. Where once all managers were from the same profession, this is no longer the case. Managers overall, whether clinical leads or departmental heads, have to have good organisation and people skills.

Usually a clinical lead has a role mixing clinic with some managerial tasks, but traditionally a manager would have an office and run a department supported by secretarial staff; running a budget, organising staff to meet the needs of the community and maintaining clinical governance standards.

Balancing priorities
>Being a manager is not about being nice to people I could be very tough when it came down to making hard decisions. I understood that the NHS is paid from the public purse. People who were off sick a lot needed help, they needed support and they needed lots of pastoral care and understanding. Managers have to deal with the constant moaning about those who were off sick, because obviously they wouldn't know what was going on in these people's lives. **Suzy Taylor**

Making a decision
> I was offered the role of manager soon after starting in podiatry, more as a team leader at first. As my career progressed I kept avoiding that road and then was asked to become Head of a new School of Podiatry. It was then I knew that I wanted to stay with a clinical role because my career was patient-led and I didn't fancy a pure managerial role as I saw it. **David Tollafield**

Becoming a manager can take you away from the clinical coalface and so for many, management may come in the form of a clinical leader role. We will see examples such as how Ian Tarr sees himself as clinical leader (diabetes) which may still mean he has to run a budget of sorts. Jill Halstead-Rastrick has clinical responsibility as well as being a manager (research). Suzy Taylor contextualises the skills required in clinican management roles.

Leadership as a consultant
> You have to be management, clinical, and a leader. Leadership and management are two completely different things, and this is where people get confused. They think it's the same thing. They're poles apart. Being a manager enables you to be effective in your job, organise everything so that it runs smoothly for the patient, but being a leader is facilitating people to develop and to learn. The women have got to be prepared to put themselves forward where the pool is small. Women need to embrace the opportunities there as much as the men. **Suzy Taylor**

A good manager should try to achieve the best delivery of health. NHS managers have to work within the framework of NHS bureaucracy. The role may be attractive to some, but be prepared for meetings. Most managers at a higher structural level have little clinical contact. In this respect there is loss in clinical skills over time.

While your career might limit your aspirations toward podiatry, many podiatrists have decided to take management further and run larger departments to include other professionals, including advising government regarding health policy, or becoming a department head. A degree in podiatry opens the door and allows transferrable skills into management.

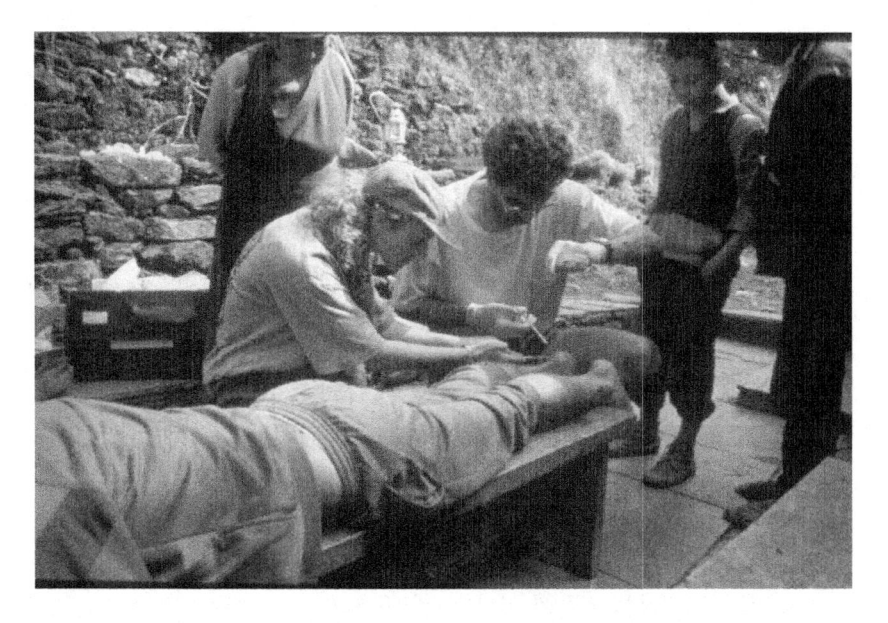

Podiatric Surgeon Dr Nat Padhiar working with a team doctor repairing an Achilles tendon at Everest. C/O Dr Padhiar

Podiatric Sports Medicine

We understand sports because the nation is attracted to football, fun runs and marathons, the Olympics, and various form of dance – and then of course we have other seasonal sports, each using different footwear and being exposed to different forms of injury.

The foot has to function and bend and take on huge forces placing each body (connective) tissue under strain. Musculoskeletal podiatry is not podiatric sports medicine and does not equate to a sports specialist.

> Everything we do has a degree of mechanics - even the diabetic foot. The diabetic foot has mechanical manifestations as does rheumatoid, because any foot deformity or disease process that you deal with in the lower limb is based around the musculoskeletal system. Podiatric sports medicine is about knowing the mechanics for each sport. Sports podiatrists are traditionally engaged with orthoses, although the specialty has become refined with re-educating sports people following injuries and encompasses a wider understanding of the whole body rather than feet alone. **Trevor Prior**

In returning to a point I have made under general podiatry and sub-specialisation; anyone can treat sports people as a podiatrist. To treat people at a higher performance level - the Olympians and professional sportsman, it is wiser to ensure further studies are taken as this area of podiatric medicine is not as it seems.

The undergraduate university courses provide a background to sports. Developing recovery programmes should ideally be managed by people who are involved with one or other sport themselves.

Limitations in professional sports

I had a call from one of the Birmingham football clubs to manage a recurrent nail problem – this was a professional player worth £x million. Despite the fact I was experienced and more than qualified, I knew the level of my professional indemnity and the fact that the team doctor dictated what I could and could not do; this made me cautious. Surgery was out of the question so I had to provide advice to keep the ailing footballer as comfortable as possible. I am not a sports specialist but as an ex-injured rugby player I understand knees intimately but that does not make me a specialist. Today my advice to any podiatrist would be never carry out treatment without the patient being made aware of the conservative options. Stay within your own area of expertise. **David Tollafield**

The Boxer

I was working in the '92 Barcelona Olympics as the podiatrist to the GB team, watching heavy weight boxing. This is different of course to dancing and tends to look at power in the upper body, stamina, lower body and the stability when using the foot and position. Watching one of the British boxers knocking the hell out of his sparring partner in the Barcelona heat in the summer, I thought, *"Goodness, the power, the punches they take to the body and to the head. It seemed ridiculous."* About an hour later the same boxer came into my surgery, knocked on the door and said, *"Simon, I need some help."* I said, *"Surely you don't need help that I can offer."* And he said, *"Well, unless you can solve this blister on my little toes, I'm not boxing for Great Britain tomorrow."* I said, *"What do you mean, this little blister?"* He took his shoe off and there was a blister that had broken. It was raw flesh. To any podiatrist, this would be a very easy problem to solve, and indeed it was. But I was surprised. I said, *"So what's stopping you? - I've been watching you knock hell out of your sparring partner, and you're saying you're not going to box for Great Britain because of your blister?"* He said, *"The pain from the blister was far greater than being smacked in the head by my sparring partner."* So ever since then my viewpoint has changed, giving me more respect for my ability and that of colleagues who treat marathon runners and the like. **Simon Costain** - *Independent Podiatrist*

Working with a professional football club

One of the lads got carried off. He had a knee injury. We went into the changing room afterwards. A colleague of mine observed. The player had ruptured his anterior cruciate ligament. Asked how I knew, I told him, *"Well, look at his knee. It's swollen up straightaway. If you get a cartilage injury, it swells up in the evening. If you rupture your ACL, you get haemarthrosis – you're at the sharp end."* **Trevor Prior**

Advice for students interested in podiatric sports medicine

For the student looking for a career, complete your BSc and engage with a subject that will bring as much motivation and enthusiasm as some of the other speciality areas in this career series. Running clubs and marathon events are as popular as ever and this is the place for podiatrists to kick start their interest in podiatric sports medicine. Find out the local event organisers and offer your services – mind you, don't expect to be paid. It is likely you will start off with the concept Simon described so well with the blister!

Dance and podiatry

It would be inconceivable to give an example of every sport that requires foot care. However, there is one that we can all relate to - dance. Different forms of movement have a unique place in foot health from the perspective of the growing foot. Here we can look at two examples - Irish dance and ballet.

Sean Savage and Simon Costain reveal the true cost behind dance. From a podiatry viewpoint, it brings the podiatrist into contact with an assessment of full-body movement, embracing more than just the foot and ankle.

> I remember I had a referral of a young guy who was dancing for the *'Lord of the Dance.'* He was advised to see a podiatrist. He saw my website, and came and saw me with a tendon injury on the outside of the foot. It turned out to be a peroneal tendon tear. He'd been to see a few people, and no one had diagnosed his problem. We got the scan and identified the injury. And then just by word of mouth, next I was known as the podiatrist who deals with dancers - I'm the dance expert! **Sean Savage**

Sean uses diagnostic ultrasound after he completes a whole assessment with some clinical tests. He assesses patients weight-bearing as well as non-weight bearing to see if they can load their body weight. Often, he refers to orthopaedics colleagues, depending on the need for special imaging.

> In the early days, I used to offer my service to the dance schools, the Central School of Ballet, Rambert, Royal Ballet, White Lodge (Royal ballet junior school), the English National Ballet and then the London Contemporary Dance Theatre. Podiatrists should be concerned about the type of shoe dancers wear outside their dance hours, because patients often buy rubbish footwear! Podiatrists working within MSK medicine don't just manage foot and ankle or lower limb problems, but we have a responsibility to assess competitive sportspeople and be open and honest with them even if on occasions, being frank with them may jeopardise their career. **Simon Costain**

Having worked with many dancers from a number of elite dance companies in London and the UK, Simon has experience in treating all ages and levels of dancers from beginners to the most elite principals.

Advice for students - how to specialise in dance?

The recently qualified student must have a good foundation in functional anatomy, medicine, physiology, and orthopaedic conditions. Most people who wish to enter the field of sports medicine understand human movement, with many taking postgraduate courses in Sports Science. While undergraduate university schools teach the essentials and framework of this science, those who wish to do well must go the extra mile. Having a degree or diploma alone does not always give you access to the real action.

> I advise all podiatrists interested in MSK Podiatry to firstly identify the best practitioners in their field, then work with several experienced MSK podiatrists. Learn from the most experienced practitioners. MSK podiatrists with experience in treating many different dancers are thin on the ground, but research who they are and try and work with them. In those early days, I offered my time and services with minimal financial reward as dancing is often poorly funded and some of the best dancers come from poor backgrounds, so some professional philanthropy is necessary. Spend a day a week to help the dancers with simple foot problems, using your unique skill set. Be prepared to extend your interest beyond the feet as many dancers suffer from ankle, lower leg, knee and hip knee injuries rather than just foot pain. Knowing your foot, ankle, leg, hip and spinal anatomy is important. **Simon Costain**

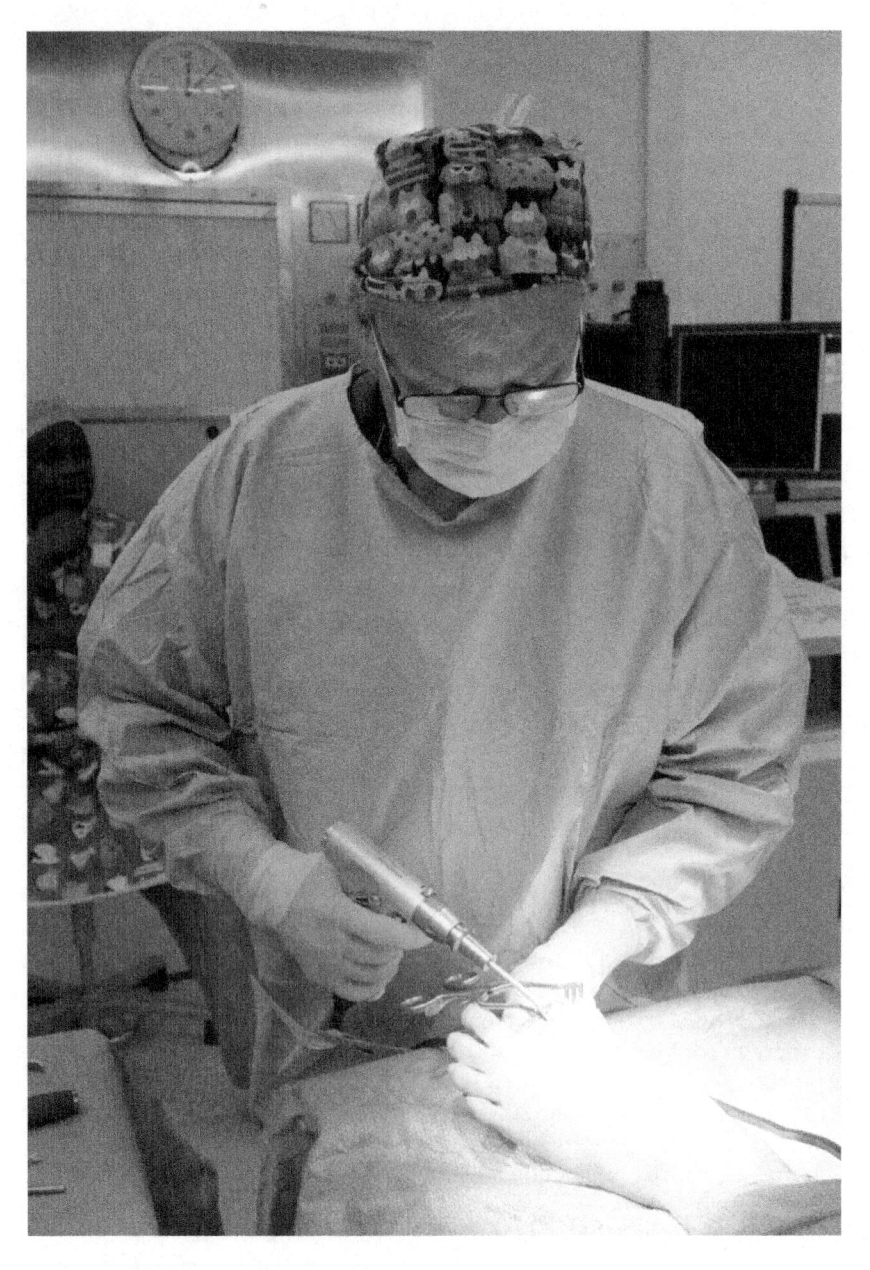

The author working with a surgical team. Specialised equipment is used to undertake bone and joint surgery

Podiatric Surgery

There is some glamour in surgery, but for most of the time it is like any other occupation; solving problems under pressure. In this section consultant podiatric surgeons provide different insights into their work.

> I was unsure of a career option with respect to podiatric surgery, and it was only in my second year after surgical rotations as a student that ignited the passion of podiatric surgery. Understanding mechanical function combined with pathology and disease is what really interested me in a career of podiatric surgery. The ability to reduce/correct deformity and the life changing results and improvements in quality of life is what attracted me to pursuing a career in podiatric surgery. **Usamah Khalid**

The medical profession originally had mixed views about non-medically trained people undertaking surgery. Influenced by high quality foot surgery from the USA podiatry brotherhood in the seventies, British podiatric surgery took off. It has never been called chiropody and so when the average British GP referred to a podiatrist, even after the name changed, they thought all podiatrists could operate. Podiatric surgery is the only area where podiatrists must take a formal postgraduate educational journey. This is the only area where a health professional can operate without a formal medical degree, apart from dentistry, on humans without medical collaboration.

> To get as far as a surgical training post means that you have to have a passion for the subject. The standard of our trainees has accelerated beyond all imagination, and the breadth and depth of knowledge and also the breadth and depth of skills that are required. Our trainees could easily hold their own against any medically trained surgical trainee. **Tim Kilmartin**

The curriculum
The principles of podiatric surgery covers a range of principles, ethics and consent associated with surgical management. Clinical assessment and investigations alongside management modules are supported by case studies and problem solving. Students use evidence around surgical management and are faced with presenting complaints to work out the appropriate management. This has the benefit of forcing them to think about the evidence linked to their assessment.

Clinical Investigations and Diagnostic Imaging is the third module covered in the first year whereby you are taught the importance of bloods results and their interpretation alongside X-Ray imaging, incorporating multiple views and to support their clinical significance. **Usamah Khalid**

Costs & prospects
No-one will advise you that a surgical career is easy. While there is a demand, placements are not always available when a podiatrist might wish to engage in this specialism. You might have a Master's in Surgery qualification but this does not guarantee a clinical (surgical) placement.

Funding of podiatric surgery – I was able to get a loan from Student Finance England to pay towards my studies at a maximum of £10,000, which was very fortunate – however, there is the option to self-fund or your employer could also sponsor the fees. Placements are not paid; however, the benefits are certainly worth it as you have the opportunity to learn from some of the very best in the profession. Challenges tend to revolve around a shortage of training positions. The Faculty of Podiatric Surgery at The Royal College of Podiatry are actively looking into this. **Usamah Khalid**

Some NHS Trusts keen on setting up surgery may pay for trainees by keeping their salary topped up. Occasionally Trusts with a surgery department will pay for posts in training. Once Fellowship is achieved there is a stronger chance to find paid employment. The state of paid surgical training therefore is by no means assured. It is easier to train whilst in NHS employment but independent podiatrists have to self-fund if no other financial support is available. **David Tollafield**

Positive changes to surgical delivery
The podiatric surgeon, as distinct from a specialist podiatrist or consultant podiatrist, is trained to be independent and, once he or she reaches consultant level, will be autonomous i.e. acts without direction. There are different levels through training from specialist podiatrist to registrar, as in the medical field, although there are no house officer posts.

Once a podiatrist has qualified and has been awarded their Fellowship, they will spend two to three more years working with distant supervision, running their own caseload as appropriate to their skills – but with a consultant on hand. Once they have completed the Certificate of Completion in Surgical Training, similarly to the medical surgeon, they can apply for a consultant post.

Current universities promoting the MSc in Surgery

Scotland's Glasgow Caledonian Univeristy and University of Huddersfield currently deliver the Master's in Podiatric Surgery programmes recognised by the Health and Care Professions Council (HCPC). The two main bodies, The Royal College of Podiatry and the Institute of Chiropodists & Podiatrists, provide clinical training through their registered members and award a Fellowship in Surgery. The NHS has a number of NHS surgical centres throughout the UK, some are training centres as well, but most reside in England.

> I completed my MSc at the University of Huddersfield, attaining a Distinction. I chose to complete it part-time across two years which allowed me to continue with clinical work and thus gain further experience; marrying theoretical knowledge to a practical and clinically-relevant caseloads. The MSc was a fantastic experience and thoroughly enjoyable. There is an expectation of increased amounts of self-directed study and lots of reading around topics, research articles and learning through conversations with peers, attending conferences aside from just reading from textbooks. There is the obvious time commitment required when undertaking such postgraduate study and sacrifice of personal time to ensure assignments are completed and OSCEs are practiced. You should be willing to work hard and have the zest for further learning. It's an excellent MSc which provides the necessary qualifications to proceed in surgical training. **Usamah Khalid**

Where does Podiatric Surgery fit in the system?

Podiatric surgery is separate from standard NHS podiatry departments or may be organised under a hospital directorate – more often this is an orthopaedic directorate. In similar ways we find that extended scope specialists (ESPs) have also separated from general NHS podiatry, more so for the diabetes podiatrist or ACP. Podiatric practitioners may be employed in different parts of the NHS. Podiatric surgery can only be delivered from a registered hospital theatre facility and has to maintain exacting standards. Many who practise podiatric surgery also work within the independent hospital system. Some podiatric surgeons work only in acute hospitals, others in community based hospitals and clinics. There are benefits to each setting and usually in the acute setting the podiatry team amalgamate with hospital staff and within a formal surgical directorate e.g orthopaedics.

What does the podiatric surgeon do?

The modern foot surgery department offers a wide range of management tools for foot pain, deformity and tissue management. The level of training emphasises diagnostic skills, use of imaging as well as surgical technique. Medicine is studied to a higher level than at undergraduate podiatry. While the aim is to avoid a foot operation, inevitably, if podiatry cannot maintain a problem, then surgery may be the only way to resolve a condition.

Podiatric surgeons mainly offer support for non-acute injury; trauma remains a specialist service under orthopaedics. Podiatrists might support chronic injury after the patient has stabilised but this could be months or years later. The role of the acute surgeon is to stabilise life first and then provide the best platform for recovery. There was the curious matter when a fellow colleague, a trauma surgeon and Head of A&E, was berated by a patient for experiencing poor nerve sensation after a serious road traffic injury. The surgeon told the dissatisfied patient after the event – *"Well at least you're alive!"*

Elective Surgery

Elective surgery is a matter of patient choice, whilst trauma surgery is a matter of need and urgency. If the foot hurts and is deformed with significant changes where footwear and conservative care cannot support the problem, then bone and joint surgery implies removal of bone, cutting and reshaping bone to improve joint function and mechanics of the foot, or replacing the joint with an artificial joint. Gross joint damage sometimes means the joint is removed and the bones have to be fixed (fused together).

Hammer toes and bunions are probably the most common conditions a podiatric surgeon sees, but nerve pain damage (*neuroma*) and complex nail bed problems may require a damaged toe to be remodelled. Some podiatric surgeons care for complex diabetic feet, others perform minor plastic surgery and reconstruction. Arthritis makes up a significant part of the foot surgeon's caseload. Training in surgical fixation requires bones to be stabilised with screws, plates and pins with a knowledge of bone grafting.

Painful flat feet may require fusions and tendon transfers, while others work in the management of sports injuries. As with any field in medicine there can only be broad definitions and the working week for a full-time

A Career in Podiatric Medicine

podiatric surgeon is long and does not follow strict hours.

Trainees & investing time
My role is to give trainees confidence. The earlier you take on podiatric surgery in your career, the better it is, the easier it's going to be for you, it rolls out easier. If you have a family, there is no doubt that in order to achieve a Fellowship in Podiatric Surgery, you will suffer, and your family will suffer as a consequence. **Tim Kilmartin**

Tim took his PhD alongside surgical training after a period teaching full time. This has enabled him to have a considerable acute perception around education of which he was one of the UK's formal leaders and the first Dean of the Faculty of Surgery when the College of Podiatry was first formed.

Training with a family
My training in Podiatric Surgery was part time. I was able to manage bringing up three children and all those things that are entailed in being a mother as well as a professional. There should not be any women out there who think that they can't do this because they want to have a life as well as a career. More and more employers are becoming progressive in terms of the way they treat equal rights for women. I think the oldest patient I've operated on was 98, and then she came back to me when she was 102. Both were minor procedures to enable her to get her shoes on and walk as far as the shops. At the other end of the scale, a dance student of 18, had a Tailor's bunion, and couldn't get her pointe shoes on. I operated, enabling her to continue her training. **Claire Freeman.**

Claire started out as a specialist podiatrist at Lewisham Hospital. Her role was to support the podiatric surgeons and to specialise in the local anaesthetic blocks to prepare patients for surgery. She needed how to learn everything, especially how to how to deliver advanced anaesthetic techniques, through to supporting the junior trainees and ensuring the relevant X-rays were available. She would assist in theatre and by the time she was practising as a consultant her role increased and she became a tutor.

From Rheumatology to Surgery
There's always been that relationship that I've had with rheumatologists. I think, on the whole, they've often been disappointed by the quality of foot surgery carried out by their orthopaedic colleagues, and they had found (*at the time*) that orthopaedics weren't that interested in the foot. **Steve Kriss**

Steve started his surgical training whilst working at the Royal Free Hospital in London and the Royal Berkshire Hospital in Reading, practising both podiatry and acupuncture. Making the change and developing surgery led to his Fellowship through the Royal College of Podiatry. His work is a mixture of private and NHS contract work, typical of many podiatric surgeons' workload.

When Tony applied to the local private hospital after becoming a consultant his hospital manager saw the value of podiatric surgery. When the outgoing Chair, a dermatologist, finished his time as Medical Advisory Chair (MAC), Tony stepped into his shoes. Becoming Chair of an MAC as a non-medical surgeon was a first for the podiatry profession.

The Independent Sector and Surgery
> My stability in the hospital depended on two things. Firstly, being good at what I do and secondly belonging to the MAC. I've now been on the MAC for a long time and have always tried to get on with people as an individuals. **Tony Wilkinson**

When Ben was approached by a consultant to join in the diabetic foot clinic, he jumped at the chance. His talents were recognised to assist with many conditions traditionally carried out by the orthopaedic team. Those months spent overseas came to pay off.

Part of an orthopaedic department
> As far as I'm concerned, it's all about your experience and your knowledge, and if you have expertise in those areas and competence in those areas, then that's something that can be expanded. I don't think the consultant who supported me probably quite envisaged that I would go as far as I have done. But, still, fair play to him, he was very much driven by it being all about your ability and your competence and if you've got competence and ability in those areas, then that's fair enough. **Ben Yates**

Expert Witness and Podiatry

Financial settlements and complaints follow all occupations although the podiatric surgeon deals with the higher end of the risk spectrum. We now meet another podiatric surgeon, Barry Francis, who specialised in expert witness work. Undertaking medico-legal work as an expert podiatrist 'witness' may be lucrative but it is not for the faint-hearted.

In the early 1970s, Barry Francis was approached by a solicitor. He remembered being quite nervous for the wrong reasons. The solicitor had a client who'd been operated on. The lady was employed by a company to clean office telephones. As part of her uniform, she had to wear court shoes.

She had a correction to a toe which resulted in the loss of her digit following an infection. She could no longer wear court shoes and, as a result of her surgical complication, she lost her job. This was a humble lady, living in East London, in not a very comfortable financial situation. As a result, she sought help from a solicitor. Her case was resolved in court, and Barry suspected that this was the first medical-legal case in which a podiatrist was involved, in a London court, before a presiding judge.

> I was up against a very senior consultant and his registrar. Unfortunately, it turned out that the consultant had been at Cambridge with the judge, which worried me somewhat. I was cross-examined the whole day by a barrister. At the end of that day I felt as if I'd been through a wringer. The case went on for several days. To my astonishment we won and the patient received damages of £28,000. **Barry Francis**

Barry felt the poor lady deserved justice, and he thought she'd been very poorly treated. He added without any sense of hubris how his contribution had changed the lady's life. Today one of the most crucial parts of defending our position as a clinician is to maintain good treatment notes. A departure from this discipline can be punitive. The earlier case of the lady who serviced telephones was won because of poor records and misleading evidence.

Becoming a Witness

> I would prefer personally to say that anybody providing an expert witness service should be at the level of - and I know that it's not appropriate in all fields - but should be occupying a post at the level of consultant. Certainly, this applies within the surgical field, it's easier when you have reached the level of a consultant because medical-legal work involves a great deal of clinical experience. **Barry Francis**

Professor Wes Vernon, forensic podiatrist on site collecting evidence

Forensic Podiatry

Like every podiatrist undertaking research, Professor Wesley Vernon, gravitated to a higher level of responsibility. He has led in the field of forensic podiatry. Podiatrists act as add-ons in the world of forensics like the forensic odontologists (dental) and part of all the other experts brought in as and when required. It's certainly rewarding but highly responsible work. Expert witness work differs from the work of the forensic scientist but still works for the courts.

Force plates to measuring pressures

One man was examined in a prison. After an hour and a half with him trying every trick in the book to elude the technique, his concentration lapsed and Wes was rewarded with one footprint.

> Most people are usually very cooperative; they might try and scrunch their feet up or make a partial print, but what we do is have at the very least two observers and occasionally more. We'll set up floor level video recordings so we can record how that footprint was left. So, if there are any anomalies, if the observers haven't picked it up - the observers would have a look at each print as it's left and instantly mark whether they agree that was an okay footprint or not. And then you look at the footage afterwards to capture the micro detail, what really happened, and ask if there is anything I might have missed.

Wes points out to date that there is a special advisory group within the Royal College of Podiatry.

> Forensic stuff is outside what podiatrists are initially trained to do. Yes, there are things we do that podiatrists could carry out, but this is forensics. Everybody was happy to pass training over to the Chartered Society of Forensic Sciences to manage the registration scheme and to the forensic regulator to recognise if there was a problem and deal with that accordingly. Most people don't do that amount of casework. I was supported by the forensic organisation. They allowed me to develop as a specialist and released me for as much as it took. **Wes Vernon**

For most people, forensic podiatry is not a full-time career so at other times they will be working in their own particular sphere of practice with maybe half-a-dozen cases a year. Forensic data analysis is labour intensive,

A Career in Podiatric Medicine

scrutinising small details of shoes and video clips. By the time Wes retired he had been involved in 800 cases which he considers unusually large.

Doubtless, Professor Wes Vernon has taken the field of forensic podiatry to an exciting level, one just waiting for younger podiatrists to come along and build on his formidable success. The development of podiatry continues to expand, but relies on those able to see the greater potential in newer fields. If there is no blueprint, then why not establish one?

The Educationalist

It is unlikely that many students immediately jump at the idea of teaching podiatry, but as a career there is much to be gained.

Motivation is the key
> I know it's very cliché, but even though I'm a full-time lecturer, every single day is very different. And I think that's what's quite satisfying about the profession. **Grace Parfitt**

Going stale
> I confess after my first seven years I had hit that seven-year itch that they say you experience in marriage! Becoming a full-time lecturer at a vibrant institution re-energised me. I needed to recharge my career if I was going to push myself further. This led to me to research lectures, take a degree and work with a team. I was also fortunate that I was able to establish a surgical unit within the local NHS hospital. **David Tollafield**

Clinician to educationalist
> Podiatry is quite a hands-on profession which I liked. It was flexible in the sense that as a podiatrist you could be employed in the health service and work privately, or you could do a mixture of the two. It also travelled well and there was the opportunity to work abroad which I liked the idea of at the time. Eventually, I spent two years working as a senior clinician in a hospital in Singapore which was a great experience. I had never really thought about university teaching, I kind of fell into it, however, it has been enjoyable seeing the students you have trained becoming successful practitioners. **Raymond Robinson**

Raymond was originally employed to work in the clinic to train students and did little lecturing. But as time went on, of course, he ended up teaching most subjects including MSK and Surgery.

> I wanted to know more than the people that I was trying to bring on. If I'm trying to advise them or coach them, then I need to have trodden that pathway too. And I think that is really what my future pattern was when I look back. **Cathy Bowen**

Cathy wanted to push the profession, promote advanced skills and bring on people with more qualifications as the degree programmes started to develop within each school. Her inner sense of progress took her to a philosophy that pushed her.

Entry to an educational career

The expectations within education are set at a high standard. You will require a degree, if not a Master's, to be accepted into a Health Sciences Faculty or Division. Full-time university lecturers will be expected to undertake research, write papers, publish and have a PhD. In the latter case, the postgraduate education is supported by the employer. The culmination of efforts and success is to have a professorship or a Chair at a university. Today podiatry has a number of professors and many PhD academics.

Working experience

Industrial work is encouraged and so there is overlap between clinical work and educational delivery. Lecturers will specialise in subjects and develop these as well as be expected to teach and lecture on other courses. The role of a lecturer is wider than many might believe. A need to communicate is essential. The role means being able to deliver course curricula, speak at conferences and promote the university institution in the UK or abroad. Tutorials, setting coursework, writing and marking examination papers are all part of the requirements that often take you beyond your formal working hours.

Education constantly changes

No profession or educational method remains the same forever, the podiatric educationalist has to change to meet different demands being made to healthcare delivery, course funding and employment requirements. Doubtless, the pendulum-style swing will ever be present, but the student who is keen on teaching will always find a rewarding career as a clinical educator.

> There's no doubt that the clinical educators play a really important role. In Glasgow, most clinical educators had full-time posts within the Department of Podiatry at the Queen Elizabeth University Hospital and their primary role is to provide clinical education to undergraduate and postgraduate students. Most clinical educators have their own sub-speciality i.e. Podiatric Dermatology, Podiatric Sports Injuries or diabetic foot management. As you become more specialised or develop a specific academic or research interest, your

field of practice narrows. That's just one of the downsides of becoming a more research-based profession. I was always keen as a Head of Department, that academic staff retained their clinical specialism. Consequently, we all had our own clinics which we ran; either one session or two sessions per week. I worked in the outpatient department in the diabetes centre located within the Queen Elizabeth University Hospital for over 25 years. Clinical care was provided by a multidisciplinary team which kept me at the top of my clinical work. I think it's important to realise, when the student comes to a clinic with you, they see the academic side, but they also see the clinician at the same time. **Stuart Baird**

Podiatric clinical education embraces the holistic side of patients, builds on the skills necessary to allow employment in the health service or independent practice, and provides eligibility for working in the industrial field. There are companies that offer agency work to full employment with Shuropody, or associateships within established independent practices. Podiatrists take on research to ensure podiatry evolves and responds to the gaps in the healthcare market. Educational opportunities are valuable and some of the best lecturers and teachers already have a wealth of industrial knowledge before becoming full-time educationalists.

Promoting podiatry

We provide taster days for students from local colleges with a series of hands-on activities. One of the activities includes handling a 'Plaster of Paris' cast of a foot. One student realised she wanted to be a plaster technician. She had no idea that that sort of job existed, and I think that's amazing. If you've found what you think you'd like to do, then I think the day is a success. If you haven't seen, or your relative hasn't seen a podiatrist, your chances of knowing about many health professions are tiny. **Simon Otter**

We stepped it up another level within podiatry, and spent a good six or eight months visiting schools in our local area and further afield, to give students an idea of what the profession is; really to let them know that it's there. Having attended a lot of events we found few students seemed to have a good grasp of what the podiatry profession was about and what we do as clinicians, other than it might be something to do with feet. **Phil Hendy**

Phil believed that the real take-home message for him was that people didn't know about podiatry. Part of his role is to push out to school-age leavers. He felt that the university needed a greater presence in careers fairs, and probably even more so at an earlier age.

Focus on health education

Phil Hendy believes it is important for students to work alongside existing clinicians so they can start to understand the differences and the nuances of the types of communication skills that they'll need to develop in order to ascertain the correct information from their patients from that kind of virtual setting.

Keri Hutchinson teaches at Cardiff Metropolitan University and took a Master's in Public Health, but has worked in acute care for 20 years within the NHS. Her interest is teaching health education, behaviour change and public health in general. In terms of her clinical role she covers all aspects of logistics.

Communication and the patient

As part of their clinical development, students have to learn how to interface with the family GP. To do this they are taught presentation skills, how to write letters or communicate by 'phone. With good lines of communication the relationship with a podiatrist will make the GP think of podiatry over other services. Her tutorials look at public health and she will focus on health inequalities and how podiatrists can be involved more in patients' lives.

Keri believes skills in communication are important. The average podiatry consultation is around about 20 minutes, twice that of the GP. She points to the importance of making communication a firm focus on how we talk to patients. The undergraduate course tries to bringing in motivational interviewing so that every contact counts. That co- productive approach fits the models within the healthcare environment so that patients open up more - taking action to change behaviour patterns in patients.

Research as a Career

BSc level

Research study projects ideally involve patients but do not have to. Building sufficient study numbers during the short period of a student's attendance at university makes the process difficult. The third-year dissertation provides an exposure to the research process. This mirrors the same process for a Master's or PhD degree, but there is a greater emphasis on reading scientific literature so the projects are inevitably based around a smaller scale project for the BSc degree.

> I didn't want to be a nurse because I just thought that was hard work and I wasn't bright enough to be a doctor. You couldn't really apply for money then, and when I asked for study leave they negotiated half that as annual leave for two years. It wasn't seen as an important role, but I was determined I was going to do it anyway. **Lisa Farndon**

Dr Lisa Farndon pushed herself up the usual career ladder. Having already qualified in podiatry she took more academic qualifications and ended up looking at the subject of epidemiology – the study of disease trends within the population. Lisa described how a previous manager – who was a podiatrist – and didn't attach importance to research. And so Lisa had to self-fund her Master's degree.

Lisa worked alongside consultant diabetologist, Dr Keith Sands, in the Diabetes Centre, who became her mentor. The ethos behind changing one's professional standing comes from not only being able to speak the language of medicine, which all podiatrists can do, but to have sufficient ability at interpreting research papers. In this regard there is a language that sets us apart. A project might fail because the design is faulty.

> When I was doing my Master's I had to read so many research papers about the diabetic foot, this led to many debates with Dr Sands and other colleagues in the multidisciplinary foot care team about all the reasons why we needed to do it one way rather than the other. We provided diabetic foot training for practice nurses and district nurses and GPs attended. They're always stunned to find how much we do and what we know. And they really enjoy it because they don't know a lot about it in general practice, only the basics. **Lisa Farndon**

The PhD Process

Tim Kilmartin, now Professor Kilmartin, was one of the first podiatric surgeons to take his studies to PhD level.

> Over the years I have published more than 80 papers. Once you have gained research skills it should then be a lifelong quest to continue looking for research questions to explore. Podiatry, like all professions, is a lifetime of learning and what better way to direct that learning than really getting on the inside of a condition or a technique, first with the literature review, then with the study design and then with the original thinking required to formulate a discussion of your findings. **Tim Kilmartin**

Lisa points out that you need to work clinically for a while and identify the area that you're interested in.

> Selecting something that you love is important because the PhD process is a long haul. Podiatrists should start small where they have not undertaken research before. Sheffield Teaching Hospitals NHS Foundation Trust has a five day evidence-based practice course which is available to all clinical staff and gives an insight into research. A small project can spark people's interest in research. Then we try and get clinicians involved in portfolio studies. Obviously not everyone needs to be a researcher. It's quite good to have one or two in a service. **Lisa Farndon**

Lisa is perhaps best known for her published work on evidence-based practice where she has taken data from clinical podiatry to look at what drives the profession, if not what defines the case load. She talks about a common problem experienced by many - the intractable plantar keratoma

(IPK) often better known as a corn. Her research led her to consider the current approaches with a grant of £250,000.

> We had one guy in the clinic in his 30s with a really nasty IPK he had suffered for years. After treatment, for the first time, he'd been able to race his son down the road and run and not have his feet hurting. The condition had affected his job as he was in pain all the time and this had affected his quality of life. We used to say we were maintaining people's foot health and as part of my PhD we called it sustaining foot health because we were stopping people from deteriorating. **Lisa Farndon**

Conditions that may appear simple and basic to some impact many in ways that don't just affect the foot, but the whole body and their social and occupational life. We recall Simon Costain's story of the boxer with a blister! Podiatry can impress others in the way we can contribute to the overall, holistic care of our patients. Research impacts all professions.

> Leadership in the NHS with an academic background is important. I will be the only person in my Trust with a PhD and this in itself is important. **Jill Halstead-Rastrick**

Jill Halstead-Rastrick has academic credentials. She decided not to go in for full-time teaching as she is passionate about clinic and has a position of clinical lead un the NHS. This rather marries research, clinical and management together. She believes she can influence change with clinical evidence, and such evidence is provided by research as a level that has kudos and is taken seriously.

Professor Tim Kilmartin took his PhD before becoming a surgeon and this has similarly made a difference to his practice as he concentrates on evidence-based care around scientific study. Helen Branthwaite specialises in footwear, building evidence for managing her patients.

There are a growing number of podiatrists who strive toward the higher academic stratosphere and although Lisa Farndon, Jill Halstead-Rastrick, Helen Branthwaite and Tim Kilmartin work in entirely different fields of podiatry they have retained a strong clinical work pattern.

6 - Closing Notes and helpful stuff

Despite packing in as much as possible into this small book, there are doubtless questions raised about a career in podiatry and the routes of entry. I hope that my colleagues and I have been able to put many myths to bed. Rather than giving too little information, I have set out to do the opposite. One of the reasons for this is that it enables a graduate to take the content further. My belief has been that no-one has ever attempted to compile all the areas of our work into one place. I hope that, if nothing else, this book will be welcomed as a valued reference.

To add to the complexity of choice, many universities are developing courses with different entry criteria. This implies you may enter a course at different times, not just entering podiatry after school with A levels. At present this book does not cover T levels (see link below), being a new form of school qualification, but this may well become wider in time.

https://tlevelinfo.org.uk/?utm_source=Search&utm_medium=CPC&utm_campaign=Agree&utm_content=AdWords

While I know my own profession well, and indeed have taken a certain liberty to add my two-penny worth, I have learnt an enormous amount about podiatry myself. Once we all were pretty much the same people – essentially undertaking the same typoe of work. Today just look at the variation in practices and types of management. This truly is a profession that has not stood still. For me, the sheer variation of roles and titles is mind boggling and if you struggle, I can assure you, you are not alone. My colleagues and I wish you well in your endeavour to find the right health career and hope in someways you won't ignore a wonderful occupation, which in my view provides employment for life.

Helpful information and resources

The following information might be useful in regard to the two professional bodies, both having websites and contacts.

The Royal College of Podiatry [https://rcpod.org.uk]
The Institute of Chiropodists & Podiatrists [https://iocp.org.uk]

Both the RCoP and IOCP provide membership with a wide variety of support and indemnity for clinical practice and have a regular publication. There are other member organisations supporting clinical practice, such as OSGO being newer, but OSGO has a narrower function. SMAE has entered the arena offering opportunities for foot health practitioners to convert to podiatrists. As indicated under Scotlands QMU, there is now collaboration enabling conversion to a 4 year BSc (Hons) Podiatry, with a HE Dip Assistant Practitioner (Podiatry) exit after completion of 2 years.

All three organisations hold clinical meetings, some being held as virtual meetings while the RCoP and IOCP hold regional branches for local members. The RCoP is the largest of the three membership groups. The RCoP runs a number of conferences each year, including one specifically for podiatric surgeons, the other for the whole membership covering a wide range of specialties.

An annual retention fee is paid each year and all podiatrists must register with the Health and Care Professions Council (HCPC) and pay an annual fee.

Associations with medicine

The Faculty of Podiatric Medicine within the Royal College of Physicians and Surgeons of Glasgow is a worldwide community of health professionals working together to improve patient care. The Faculty was established in 2012 - recently celebrating its 10-year anniversary - and attracts clinicians from around the world, with Fellows and Members from over 20 different countries. Membership is open by application to all experienced HCPC Registered Podiatrists with an outstanding record of clinical podiatric medicine.

The global need for clinical excellence in treating conditions of the foot is increasing dramatically. The Faculty is committed to supporting podiatrists through education, training and continuous professional development throughout all career stages.

The Health and Care Professions Council can be found at https://www.hcpc-uk.org

There is a useful reference to universities in general and you can also check the current AfC pay scales for NHS employment.

> How to find a podiatrist for contact experience?
> [https://rcpod.org.uk/find-a-podiatrist#FIND.PODIATRIST] – go to the website of the Royal College of Podiatrists Checked 25/10/22
>
> Which university to select?
> Rcpod.org/become-a-podiatrist/qualifying-funding 25/10/22
>
> Careers
> [https://rcpod.org.uk/become-a-podiatrist/career-opportunities-and-scope]
>
> Salaries in the NHS
> [https://www.healthcareers.nhs.uk/working-health/working-nhs/nhs-pay-and-benefits/agenda-change-pay-rates/agenda-change-pay-rates]

Please note all links are subject to change without notice but were accurate at the time of publication. Also, the official names for some of the job descriptions may change. In other cases some titles may overlap.

This career book can only provide the student reader with a general feel for the profession which continues to progress rapidly. All universities have a website and should be referred to to expand on any details omitted in this book.

The Glossary contains information and terms used within this book for general reference.

A&E – Accident & emergency equivalent to ER emergency room (USA)
ABPI- Short for ankle-brachial pressure index and forms a standard screening assessment for circulation quality in a limb
ACL – Anterior cruciate ligament found in the knee and important to keep the knee stable
Acute (general) hospital - A hospital usually with a full complement of support services, operating theatres and admission wards and critical care facilities. Also has an A&E department
Achilles – Largest tendon at the back of the ankle affecting foot balance made from two main muscle tendons – gastrocnemius and soleus. Named after the Greek warrior
AHP Allied Health Professional – name given to health professionals included on the HCPC register representing those who underpin healthcare.
AfC – Agenda for Change replaced the Whitley pay scales in 1983. Nursing and AHPs are remunerated on AfC scales 5-9
Anaesthetic – A pharmacological substance that blocks nerve impulses.
Anatomy – The study of the human body divided into bones, joints, ligaments, muscles, nerves, arteries & veins
Aneurysm – Ballooning of a blood vessel, often and artery
Angio-thrombosis obliterans – A rare condition that blocks vessels from blood flow causing the foot to become gangrenous (infected). May be associated with heavy smokers.
Apprenticeship scheme – A method of studying while being employed on a salary at a reduced rate and supported financially through the course
Arthritis – Damage to a joint that deteriorates. It may be inflamed or stiff in association with injury or disease

Associate clinician (podiatry) – A podiatrist may be associated with a practice but does not have a share in that practice. They are not salaried but pay into the practice an agreed sum for the use of the premises
At-risk – A term used to determine the likelihood of a patient developing a life or limb threatening problem
Audit – Data to show both activity and frequency of resources used
Autoclave – A vessel that uses steam and pressure to sterilise instruments
BAME – Black, Asian and Minority Ethnic
Biomechanics – The study of human movement broken into kinesiology (movement) and kinematics (forces).
Biopsy – Taking a sample of tissue
BSc – Bachelor of Science – the first degree level awarded by a university
Blister – Loss of the top layer of skin due to fluid build-up through friction and shear. At risk of infection and slow healing which can deteriorate. *See Epidermolysis bullosa*
Bunion – A bump on the side of the big toe but usually associated with the big toe bending towards the next toe e.g. *hallux valgus*
Bursary – A grant or sum of money available often given as an award which does not have to be paid back
Cadaver – Associated with anatomical dissection pertaining to a dead human
Cancer – Common name for abnormal cell changes. May be malignant e.g. melanoma - a cancer of cells within the skin producing melanin
Cannulation – A procedure where a needle is placed into a vein with the purpose of introducing licensed medication
Caustics – A chemical usually applied to the skin to cause controlled damage.
Chiropodist – Former name for a podiatrist but a professional who does not hold a degree in podiatry
Cellulitis – An overwhelming infection that can lead to blood poisoning and death
Clinical Governance (in healthcare) – A system of accountability for delivering a service and safeguarding standards to produce best clinical practice
Community hospital – Usually involved with day care treatment. Does not have a full set of services as an acute hospital has but may have operating theatres. Does not have emergency services but may provide minor injury support
Compartment syndrome – Fluid builds within sections of the limb called fascia causing pressure on blood vessels leading to blood supply deprivation and risk of limb loss in extreme cases
Complex regional pain syndrome – An unusual sequence of changes affected by nerves and changes in the blood vessels leading to extreme and constant pain
Connective tissue – Any tissue in the body that has a connective function, binding or supporting the skeletal framework. Typically this comprises the protein - collagen
Consultant –The highest level of clinical appointment work and usually implies a leadership and teaching role but may involve research. Consultants are not limited to surgeons or medical doctors
Continuous Professional Development - Also known as CPD is a process of adding to both skills and knowledge to an education profile or portfolio and

developed after qualifying

Core podiatry – A term used to encapsulate essential podiatric care e.g. foot health screening, first line management of the foot

Cryotherapy – the use of cold in treatment. *Also termed cryosurgery for non-invasive surgery*

Curriculum Vitae or C.V (U.S Resume) – a prepared list of professional appointments, awards, publications to chart the progress and positive professional development. A requirement for interview

Debridement – The use of sharp dissection to reduce dead tissue

Diabetes – Complex disease usually associated with insulin output within the pancreas

Diagnosis – The conclusion formed following medical examination and tests

Dissertation (thesis) – The final part of a Bachelor honours degree and requires a study using research methods that usually involves some statistical analysis

Dermatology – The formal medical term for the study of skin disease

Domiciliary - Visiting practice in a patient's home

DPM- Doctor of Podiatric Medicine - Only awarded in the USA and Canada. Not equivalent to PhD

Diversity – An awareness of social morality within a community and a key part of treating patients equally and with respect

ESP/Extended Scope Podiatrist/Practitioner – An advanced level of clinical practice in podiatry with sub specialisation in diabetes, rheumatology, surgery

ECSWT – Extra corporeal shock wave treatment – widely used for sports injuries using impulse energy on connective tissue

Elective (surgery) - Means choice and is not considered urgent or life threatening

Epidermolysis bullosa – A congenital condition affecting the skin cells which causes the top layer to shed exposing large areas to potential infection

Expert witness – A person who provides professional evidence to a legal court in a (*usually as a civil claim when associated with healthcare*) claim against a person or organisation where it is assumed negligence has arisen

Fellowship (Fellow) – An advanced level of membership. A college may bestow a clinical fellowship denoting clinical excellence and seniority in that area of specialism especially after completing examinations e.g Fellow of the Royal College; of Medicine, of Surgeons, of Podiatry etc

First Contact Practitioner – A new group of trained clinicians designed to provide wider and advanced services in the community

Fissure – A condition where the skin on the foot forms linear splits through the top layer of skin sometimes reaching the deeper level where blood vessels and nerves are exposed resulting in potential infection

Foot Health Practitioner – A body of health care workers who are not registered with the HCPC but may work under podiatrists. Their role is limited to nails and skin with some practising work with orthoses.

Forensic podiatry – Sub-specialty assisting the police and law courts.

Gender – Traditionally relates to the sex of a human but in modern health terms the definition extends to wider inclusions within society based on personality and psychological wellbeing

GMC – General Medical Council
GP - General practitioner of medicine. Family doctor and physician
GPP - General practitioner in podiatry
Hammer toe – One or more toes become bent at their knuckles so sticking up rubbing against shoes. A deformity of the foot
Health Care Professionals – A person who provides health care in the UK
H.E.E / Health Education England – A leadership organisation backed by HM Govt. supporting education, training and workforce development
HCPC –Health & Care Professions Council – statutory government body set up to ensure standards are maintained and have the power to remove a podiatrist or AHP from the register barring them from practising as an HCPC registered podiatrist
Holistic – More than just the foot but considers all aspects of health
ICATS – Integrated clinical assessment and treatment services (*NHS*)
IOCP - Institute of Chiropodists & Podiatrists
Independent Prescriber (I.P.)– Someone who has taken a course leading to training in advanced knowledge of medications usually allowed by medical doctors
Imaging – Implies any investigation usually under a radiology department run by radiographers (AHPs).
Independent practice – Non-NHS based practice which may take place in rented or self-owned buildings and can also include NHS contracts arranged to provide care usually at a set fee or remuneration
IRMER - Ionising radiation (medical exposure) regulations – a basic certification to allow health care professionals to use X-rays and other forms of imaging
Ischaemic – Loss of blood supply
Keratin – A collection of cells that exist as a top layer of the skin to protect the body from foreign materials. The tissue also involves nails
Keratolytic – A chemical that has the ability of breaking down skin cells to soften the surface – **'lysis'** means to breakdown
LASER - Light amplification by stimulation emission of radiation
Locum – Someone employed on a sessional or part time or full-time basis through a second party e.g. agency but does not work under an employment contract for the department where they are engaged to provide a service
MAC – Medical advisory committee in a hospital
Material science – The study of physics and chemistry in relation to materials e.g. leather, plastics
MD – A higher academic doctorate award in medicine in the UK but a standard award for graduating doctors in the USA
MSc - Master's Degree in Science – second degree awarded at a higher academic level
MSK/Musculoskeletal – The specific reference to the main components of the body responsible for human movement
MDT/Multidisciplinary Team – An accepted term for a group of professionals who work within a collaborative framework around a specialism.
Mycosis (mycotic) - Pertains to fungal, fungal infection

Necrotizing fasciitis - Has mixed disease features of serious infection (*clostridium and streptococcus*), fluid build-up in the compartments of the limb and loss of blood supply. A condition that leads to death or amputation
Networking – A process of communication for mutual benefit between two or more people
Neuromuscular – Affecting the branch of anatomy relating to nerves supplying muscle groups
Neuropathy – Where the nerves and pathways fail to conduct either sensation or movement. Common in infections and some diseases but also poor nutrition *e.g leprosy, uncontrolled diabetes*
Oncology – Study and branch of medicine dealing with cancer e.g. oncologist
Orthopaedics – The branch of medicine that involves the management of diseases and injury to bones and joints
Orthopaedic (surgeon) – Provides a service specialising in the musculoskeletal framework to include management of emergency trauma
Orthoses (foot orthotic) – A device that supports and stabilises the foot in order to improve function
Orthotist – A person trained to provide made-to-measure or bespoke footwear, orthoses and prosthetics
Osteomyelitis – Bone infection
Osteosarcoma – A serious bone cancer with high malignancy status
Partnership – Applied to business with an agreed percentage share of the business and responsibilities
Paediatric – Study and treatment of children. Branches of medicine may sub-specialise in paediatric care *e.g. paediatric orthopaedics, podo-paediatrics*
PGD - Patient Group Directive – a method of using prescription only medication under direction through a set protocol
Pathology – The study of how disease affects the tissues of the body and may cover microbiology. Divided into gross pathology and cellular levels.
Pedicure - Cosmetic management of nails and skin without surgery offering the benefit of making the appearance satisfying to the eye
Peroneal nerve injury – Lower limb nerve damage supplying muscles.The effect can cause the foot to drop with loss of muscle power
PhD – A doctorate – Doctor of Philosophy considered one of the highest academic qualifications. Medical doctors are not equivalent to PhD but have their own honorary doctorate. Their basic degree is MBBS Bachelor of Medicine, Bachelor of Surgery.
Podiatric Surgeon – A podiatrist qualified and registered to perform surgery beyond the skin and superficial structures. Will have a Fellowship from an official body e.g. FRCPodS Fellow of the Royal College of Podiatry (surgery)
Podiatric Medicine - The study of podiatry at BSc level embraces medicine and science and includes basic sciences, anatomy, pathology, physiology, pharmacology, medicine, orthopaedics and surgery
Podologues - European equivalent term for podiatrist especially Spain (podologo male & podologa female)
POM – Prescription only medicine available from a registered pharmacy (see

independent prescriber)
Postgraduate – A period of study after university i.e after BSc level education
Physiology – The study of how the human body works e.g. innervation of the heart and electrical conduction. Part of medical sciences
Primary care – Healthcare in the community associated with first contact medical care
Private practice – The business of a Sole Trader or Limited Company providing a service for a fee also known as independent practice
Professor –Professorships are usually given as 'seats' in a university and the individual may lead a department, will usually have a PhD, and provided academic leadership. They are the highest non-administrative academic award. *Emeritus Professor* the status is an honorary category of appointment. *e.g UCL confers the title upon retiring professors*
Prosthetic – An appliance that is made to make up for the loss of a part of the body, mainly limbs
Radiologist – Medical doctor specialising in radiology
Registration – A requirement to maintain names of qualified persons who meet statutory standards. Examples include GMC (medicine), HCPC (Allied Health Professionals). Regulated by a body appointed by Parliament.
Renal – Of the kidney
Respiratory – System relating to the lungs and human oxygenation of the blood. Closely allied to the heart e.g. cardio-respiratory function
RCoP – Royal College of Podiatry. Largest professional body of podiatry in the UK
Rheumatology – A specialism in medicine covering the MSK structure with specific reference to connective tissue and disease
RMO – Resident Medical Officer *e.g often in the independent hospitals but a senior house officer-registrar grade*
Screening – A process of examining a patient to identify changes that might lead to deteriorating health
Skill –Knowledge that allows experience and development of a competency in terms of practical ability or academic knowledge
Sports medicine – The science of study in athletes which includes nutrition, biomechanics, orthopaedics, pharmacology, imaging and features understanding all aspects of medicine and control mechanism through physiology
Steroid – A powerful drug used to suppress inflammation
Sterilise – A process where all organisms are removed by sterilisation, usually autoclave as opposed to *disinfection* where organisms may not be killed
Trench foot – Disease of the foot affecting circulation because of cold and damp together with infection
Triage – In the modern sense of layering or filtering out the urgency of care.
Thyroid – An endocrine organ found in the neck that produces a hormone thyroxine being important for regulation and homeostasis
Ulcer – Loss of the skin layer to cause a wound that may fail to heal. Sizes vary - *see ischaemic and neuropathy*
Ultrasound – Supports treatment and imaging investigation using ultrasound

wave forms. It uses no radiation and is highly useful for soft tissue management and diagnosis
Undergraduate – A student who has not been to university before
Vascular – Of the blood vessels supporting all the body organs, joints and MSK frame. Part of the cardiac (heart) system involving vein and arteries
Verruca (pedis)– A viral infection of the skin on the foot not exclusively found in children. Also known as wart
X-ray – Part of formal imaging of bones using controlled radiation

Gait analysis is an important part of a podiatrist's role. Inscribed by actor, author and comedian, John Clease who wrote to Podiatrist Simon Costain *'Simon, salutations and thanks, from the Minister of increasingly PERFECT walks.'* C/O Mr D.S Costain consultant podiatrist Gait Centre Harley Street, London

Quick History of Podiatry

For those interested, modern podiatry was derived from many sources of footcare before the 18th century, and is generally poorly documented until the 19th century. Doubtless, charlatan foot doctors existed. Formal education arose after the first Great War (1914-18). Here is a run-down of the key dates.

1846 – Lewis Durlacher wrote his treatise on the foot as Surgeon Chiropodist (to William IV and Queen Victoria)
1900s - First schools of chiropody (London Foot Hospital) introduced with medical support
1938 – Board of Registration of Medical Auxiliaries, established a voluntary register operated by the British Medical Association on a voluntary basis
1960 - The Professions Supplementary to Medicine Act – Act of Parliament formed the Council for the Professions Supplementary to Medicine.
 Diploma course extends to three years from two years. All chiropodists have to be registered to work in the NHS. The register is designed to offer standards of practice and protect the public. (See 2003)
- NHS chiropody commences with a pay structure under Whitley Council rates
1969 – the first local anaesthetic courses were run in November and December 1969 by the Croydon Postgraduate Group leading to developing nail surgery
1974 – The Podiatry Association (PA) formed a group to develop surgery with a certificate initially, then a Diploma in Podiatry leading to the first Fellowship in

foot surgery (FPodA)
1977 – Local anaesthetics and nail surgery was introduced into schools (Medicine Act changed 1980)
1978- Foot Care Assistants developed formerly by the Association of Chief Chiropody Officers (ACCO)
1980-1982 – Formation of first NHS surgery in Shropshire Mr Mike Allard-Williams FPodA
1993 - HRH Queen Elizabeth the Queen Mother becomes Patron of the College of Podiatry
1993 - The first Undergraduates qualified with a BSC – prior to that they were top-up degrees (from 1988).
1996-7 - The Podiatry Association and ACCO merge with the Society of Chiropodists & Chiropodists to form the College of Podiatry. Four Faculties form each with a Dean appointed to each Faculty.
1990 *onwards* – The title chiropodist was dropped in favour of podiatry from the formal educational qualification.
2003 – The Council for Professions Supplementary to Medicine (CCPM) became the Health and Care Professions Council (HCPC) and protected the title chiropody and podiatry from unqualified use.
2000-2003 The Master's degree for podiatric surgery and advanced podiatry education were established
2004 – Whitley rates of pay for the NHS change to Agenda for Change AfC Bands 5-9
2005   HRH Duchess of Cornwall becomes Patron to the College of Podiatry
2012 - The Faculty of Podiatric Medicine within the Royal College of Physicians and Surgeons of Glasgow
2016 - Independent Prescribing (I.P) becomes available to podiatrists
2020 - Podiatry played a formal part within the London Olympics
2021 - The College of Podiatry becomes the Royal College of Podiatry
2022 - Annotation of podiatrists practising foot surgery designated on the HCPC register for the first time alongside the independent prescribers.

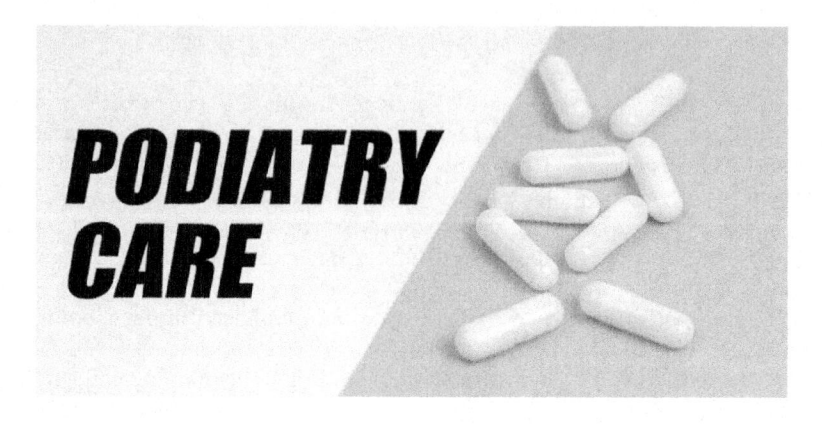

PODIATRY CARE

Ackowledgements

I am indebted to many podiatrists who have contributed their time and experience to this career book from across the United Kingdom. Gratitude goes to podiatrist Martin McGeogh who was kind enough to support this book through Firefly, and having confidence in the project. To Southampton University for rolling out the first draft edition to local schools and to Hans Bakker and Max Jenvey at Canonbury Ltd for promoting podiatry.

I am truly sorry I could not include more professionals – had I done so this book would have expanded to the size of the Encyclopaedia Britannica. I have included a separate list of the professional contributors. Every effort has been made to invite all universities to contribute or comment on the pre-published version of this book.

Many of the students I interviewed had to struggle with the effect of punitive lockdowns during the height of the Covid 19 era, but they maintained an impressive enthusiasm for this career project. Their contributions are important as they have added realism and colour to the messages. By the time of release most will have graduated and I wish them well in their future roles – *Catriona Doyle, Christine Hall, Ektaa Vadgama, Ellen McGeough, Emily Reaney, Ethan Gifford, Nancy Keller, Paul Haughian, Paul Murphy, Ryan Brain, Sarah Walsh, Shona Wesley, Shuja Merban, Zoe Alexander*

To Debbie Delves, Nat Padhiar and Nick Knight for providing additional images. A special mention should go to my proof readers and copy editors. Benjamin Jones, Jonathan Small, Nancy Calegari and Jane Clare. To Professor Cathy Bowen who tolerated my numerous e-mails and calls to assist with the rheumatology section and facilitated a group of people willing to come forward. In addition, Nancy provided all the transcribing and turned around the 70+ interviews used in these pages with incredible speed and accuracy. To my wife, Jill, as ever my guide and auricle.

Of course my greatest thanks go to the readers and colleagues – the careers teachers who have found this book useful to guide their own proteges and pass on the value hopefully intended.

Professional Contributors

University based

- Emeritus Professor Alan Borthwick, OBE University of Southampton
- Dr Andrew Bridgen, University of Huddersfield
- Professor Catherine Bowen, University of Southampton
- Mr Ben Bullen, Cardiff Metropolitan University
- Mr Benjamin Jones, University of Southampton
- Dr Grace Parfitt, University of Huddersfield
- Ms Keri Hutchinson, Cardiff Metropolitan University
- Ms Hayley Edginton, Salford University
- Professor Jackie Wakefield, Queen Margaret University, Edinburgh
- Mr Phil Hendy, Plymouth University
- Mr Raymond Robinson, Ulster University
- Mr Rodrigo Diaz-Martinez, Northampton University
- Dr Simon Otter, Brighton University
- Emeritus Professor Stuart Baird, Glasgow Caledonian University

Academic podiatrists with joint clinical posts

- Dr Heidi Siddle, Research Podiatrist
- Dr Helen Branthwaite, Independent and ResearchPodiatrist
- Dr Jill Halstead-Rastrick, Research Podiatrist
- Dr Lisa Farndon, Clinical Research Podiatrist/Research Lead

Clinical podiatrists

- Ms Afni Shah-Hamilton, Independent Podiatrist
- Ms Alison Clarke-Morris, Independent Podiatrist
- Mr Antony Wilkinson, Consultant Podiatric Surgeon, NHS
- Mr Barry Francis, Consultant Podiatric Surgeon, NHS (Rtd)
- Mr Ben Yates, Consultant Podiatric Surgeon, NHS
- Ms Catherine Holdcroft, NHS Podiatrist
- Mr Christopher Joyce, Extended Scope Podiatrist in Rheumatology at Homerton Healthcare NHS Foundation Trust.
- Ms Claire Carr, Independent Podiatrist
- Ms Claire Freeman, Consultant Podiatric Surgeon, NHS
- Mr Damian Holdcroft, Extended Scope Podiatrist, Orthopaedics
- Ms Debbie Delves, Independent Podiatrist

- Ms Edwina Alcock, Advanced Practice Podiatrist MSK, NHS
- Ms Emily Haworth, Specialist Podiatrist in Diabetes
- Mr Ganesh Baliah, Podiatrist
- Mr Karl Guttormsen, Advanced Clinical Practitioner in Diabetes, Endocrinology & Gen. medicine
- Mr Ian Tarr, Extended Scope Podiatrist in Diabetes Community Walsall
- Dr Ivan Bristow, Podiatrist with special interest in Dermatology
- Mr Jai Saxelby, Independent Podiatrist
- Mr James Welch, Advanced Specialist Podiatrist (MSK & Paediatrics)
- Ms Jennifer Muir, Independent Podiatrist
- Ms Jessica Warner, Podiatrist
- Mr Jonathan Small, Independent Podiatrist
- Ms Judith Watson, Independent Podiatrist
- Ms Louise Kennedy, Independent Podiatrist
- Mr Martin Fox, Specialist Podiatrist
- Mr Ralph Graham, Consultant Podiatric Surgeon, NHS (Rtd).
- Ms Sarah Twiss, NHS Podiatrist
- Mr Sean Savage, Independent Podiatrist
- Ms Siobhan Muirhead, Podiatrist
- Mr Simon Costain, Podiatric Surgeon & Consultant in Gait Analysis
- Mrs Stephanie Owen Independent Podiatrist MSK specialist
- Mr Steve Kriss, Consultant Podiatric Surgeon, NHS
- Ms Suzy Taylor, Consultant Podiatric Surgeon, NHS
- Professor Tim Kilmartin, Consultant Podiatric Surgeon, NHS
- Mr Trevor Prior, Consultant Podiatric Surgeon, NHS
- Mr Usamah Khalid, Podiatrist
- Ms Victoria North, Independent Podiatrist
- Professor Wesley Vernon. OBE (Rtd), University of Huddersfield.

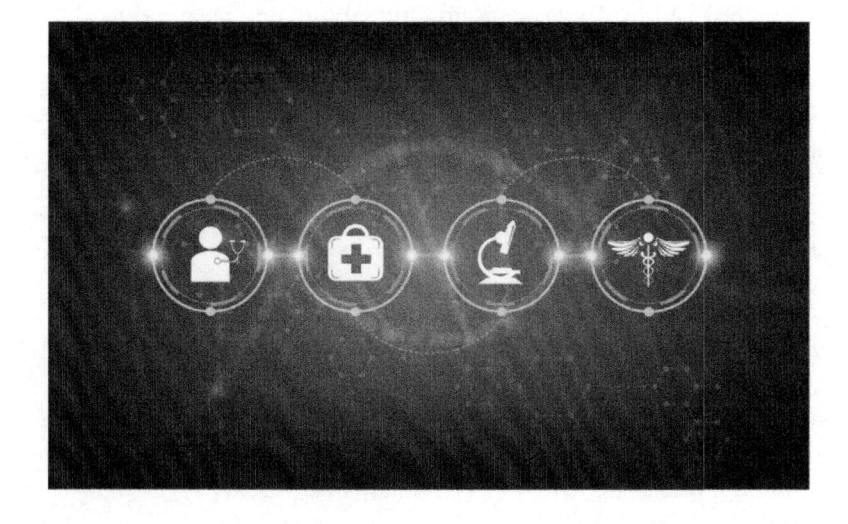

About the author

David qualified in 1978 from the London Foot Hospital (University of College Hospital) - one of the few funded NHS training centres.

He has worked in most fields of podiatry before it changed from the older term chiropody. After seven years in clinical practice he became Deputy Head of School and senior lecturer at Nene College (*now Univeristy of Northampton*) where he supported the new school from 1985 with Head of School, Linda Merriman. They produced two principle texts for podiatry students for the new degree course between 1995 and 1997.

David completed his surgical fellowship in 1986 and established the first integrated student course with foot surgery collaborating between Nene College and Northampton General Hospital.

By 1995 he returned to the NHS to become a full-time consultant podiatric surgeon and continued teaching undergraduates and postgraduates in podiatry. He spent the remainder of his career in the West Midlands working with the community NHS until he joined the orthopaedic directorate in 2012 at the Manor Hospital, Walsall.

He left the NHS in 2014 and worked at Spire Little Aston Hospital until retiring from full clinical practice in 2018.

He continues with research, educational talks and writing about podiatric medicine and practice. To date he has published a number of research papers, articles and books.

During his career he has held various professional posts; Council member of the former Royal College of Podiatry (1997-2000) and Dean of Faculty of Podiatric Surgery (2012-2014). He has travelled widely lecturing in South Africa, New Zealand, Israel, Finland, USA and Eire as well as the UK.

He currently holds an affiliate staff membership at the University of Huddersfield. David is married with four children and five grandchildren and is keen on military history and amateur dramatics.

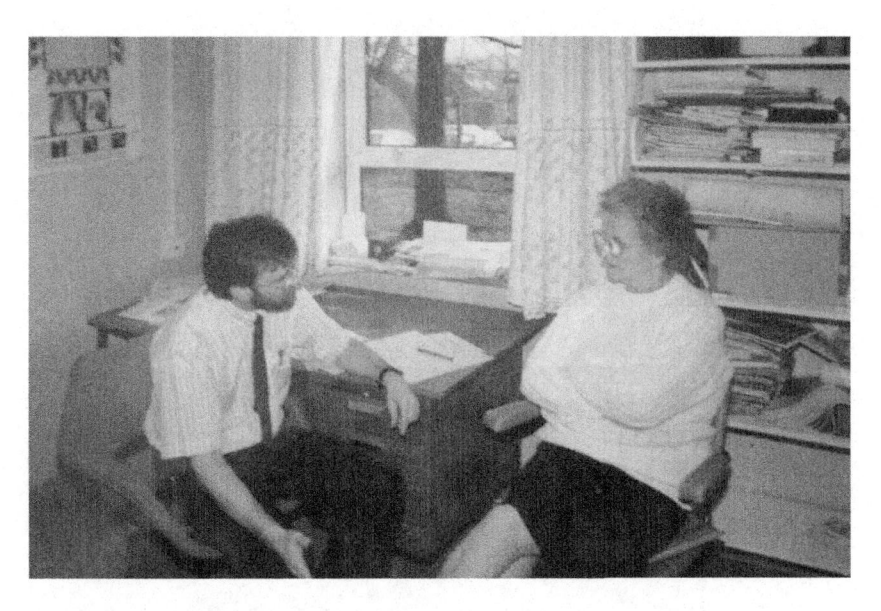

Early days as a Consultant with patient at the Manor Hospital, Walsall, old outpatient department

Useful Career books from the author
Step into podiatry as a career

Voices from Podiatric Medicine
Coming later in 2023 and available at Amazon books

Alongside this career book you can read the companion, *Voices from Podiatric Medicine, Career Journeys Past & Present*, written and created with the support of 30 authors and colleagues who have contributed to this book. Their stories are told in full and take you on some wonderful journeys home and abroad. From house calls to the field of dermatology, forensic science, sports medicine, foot surgery and research – podiatry covers a broader field of work than you might imagine.

Podiatrist on A Mission

Tales from the author's own memoirs takes the reader back in time to the commencement of podiatry reinforced by a mission containing twists and turns from Northampton to San Francisco and back. Meet his patients and his colleagues as his story unfolds.

"For me, it was a page turner... a very easy read with an underpinning of extensive knowledge. Brilliant." *Alison Charlton*

"As a novel I simply loved reading your story. There are highs and lows, laughter and tears and your drive and humility were well matched to get you through." *Janet McGroggan*

"Thoroughly entertaining, I found it very easy to read and enjoyed it immensely." *Rob Hardy*

Foot Health Myths, Facts and Fables

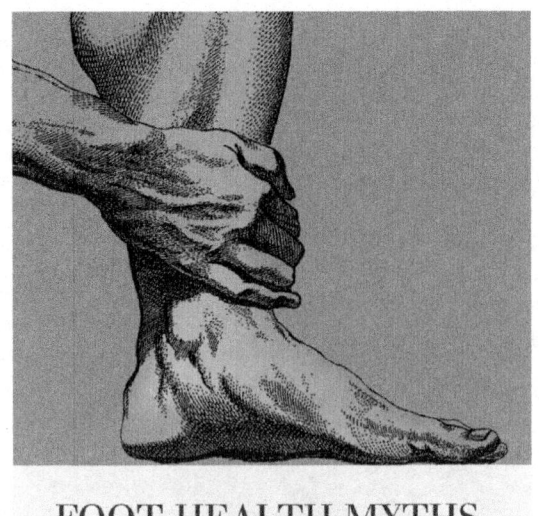

FOOT HEALTH MYTHS, FACTS & FABLES

Podiatry Reflections

David R Tollafield

Whilst waiting to take up podiatry at university, the author was provided with perhaps the most unhelpful information imaginable that could have led to him taking another career. After a wonderful career in podiatric medicine, David, podiatrist turned author, writes the book all students should have had while awaiting to start university.

"...this book is beautifully conceived and flows with questions and answers at a level I can understand and everything is explained very clearly... It is engaging and accessible without dwelling too long on anything... that doesn't talk down to me, not trying to impress, not dry and boring." *Shaun   Global*

"This is a fascinating book stuffed with an abundance of facts, supported by figures and data engrossing historical references, together with the origins of medical terminology, make for enlightened reading." *Sid Gibson*

More books by the same author

Unless mentioned, all books are available through Amazon books

Non-fiction

Foot Health Myths, Facts and Fables
Podiatrist on A Mission
Selling Foot Health as Podiatry
Projecting Your Image. Conference to Village Halls
PowerPoint is More than a Slide Program
Bunion Hallux Valgus. Behind the Scenes
Morton's Neuroma. Podiatrist Turned Patient: My Own Journey

With Linda Merriman

Published under Churchill-Livingstone

Clinical Skills in Treating the Foot
Assessment of the Lower Limb

Fiction

Fatal Contracts
shocking short stories with a sizzling sting in the tale

*****

The Story of Crystal Rouge*
(A children's story about an ink pen and colour prejudice)

Only available directly from the author
Busypencilcasecfp@gmail.com

Index

A

Achilles tendon 97
Acupuncture 188
Acute hospitals 185
Advanced Clinical Practitioner (ACP) 32, 165
Afc6 39
Afni Shah-Hamilton 32, 122, 144,145, 172, 214
Agency work 196
Agenda for Change 16, 79, 128, 204, 212
Alison Clarke-Morris 214
All Party Parliamentary committees in the Houses of Parliament.. 143
Allied Health Professionals (ahps) 23
Amputation rates 148
Anatomy. 17, 20, 22, 53, 56, 62, 65, 69, 70, 77, 160, 181, 208
Anatomy 22, 24, 62, 204
Andy Bridgen 87, 88, 128
Aneurysm 141, 142, 153
Antibiotics 59, 88, 122, 166
Apprenticeship scheme 101, 104
Areas of special interest 109, 122
Associate Podiatrist 164
At Risk Podiatry 145
Australia 83, 92, 159

B

Bacteria 93
Ballet 181
Barcelona Olympics 178
Barrister 190
Barry Francis 55, 189, 214
Ben Bullen 63, 83, 84, 213

Ben Yates 19, 188, 214
Biology 51, 62
Biomechanics 10, 22, 50, 55, 56, 84, 116, 120, 123, 129, 132, 150, 156, 158, 159, 160, 161, 209
Biopsy 120, 122
Blisters 35, 119, 124, 156, 178-9
Blood flow 139
Blood pressure 72, 111, 141
Boxing 178
Building confidence 115
Bullying types 100
Bunion 221
Bursaries 101
Business coach 158
Business development 37
Business management 52
Business partnership 122
Buying books 106

C

Cadaver classes 69
Calcutta 94
Callus 21, 118, 119, 120
Care homes 126
Career plan 113, 115
Cartilage injury 179
Cathy Bowen 88, 149, 194, 213
Catriona Doyle 18, 74, 213
Certificate of completion in surgical training 184
Chartered Society of Forensic Sciences 192
Children 83, 84
Chris Joyce 147, 148, 150, 214
Chronic pain 147, 152
Claire Carr 10, 35, 98, 158, 164, 173, 214
Claire Freeman 187, 214

Clubfoot 94
Communication skills 47, 72, 77, 197
Computer 19, 45, 121, 157
Connective tissues 49, 55
Continuous professional development 87, 115, 202
Continuous Professional Development (CPD) 27
Core podiatry 156, 206
COVID 74, 142
Crime series 36
Cryotherapy 26, 120
Current salaries 131
Curriculum 3, 14, 25, 50, 61, 62, 80, 83, 91, 183
Cyclists 75, 161

D

Damian Holdcroft 134
Dance/dancers 15, 35, 97, 177, 180, 181, 187
David Tollafield . 16, 35, 39, 72, 77, 92, 113, 117, 126, 153, 170, 176, 178, 184, 194
Debbie Delves 171, 172, 214
Debridement 54, 206
Debriding wounds 40
Dental suites 122
Dermatology 85, 195, 206, 214
Dermatoscope 85, 124
Dexterity 34, 54
Diabetic 18, 34, 47, 59, 60, 114, 116, 128, 135, 137, 139, 141, 142, 146, 147, 148, 154, 157, 177, 185, 186, 188, 195, 199
Diabetic wounds 47
Dissertation .61, 66, 67, 73, 74, 198
District nurse 121, 154
Domiciliary 28, 125, 126

Doppler equipment 142
Dynamic taping 123
Dyslexia 22, 45

E

Edwina Alcock 132, 133
Ektaa Vadgama 47, 70, 213
Elective surgery 186
Electrocautery 122
Ellen McGeough 22, 47
Emily Haworth 137, 138, 214
Emily Reeney 22, 47, 74, 97, 213
Enucleate corns 118
ERASMUS programme 92
Ethan Gifford ... 21, 47, 59, 74, 213
Expert witness 36, 55, 167, 190, 192
Extended Scope Practitioner 31, 128
Extra corporeal shock wave therapy 80

F

Faculty of Podiatric Medicine (*Royal College of Physicians and Surgeons of Glasgow*) ... 202, 212
First Contact Practitioner ... 32, 165, 206
Foot Health Practitioners 30, 118
Foot protection team 136
Foot surgery ... 31, 71, 94, 153, 183, 186, 187, 212
Football clubs 35, 178
Footwear design 161
Forensic podiatry 36, 191
Fun runs and marathons 177

G

Gait (walking) 120
Gait Analysis Shoe Prescription (GASP 157

Gait laboratories 56, 173
Ganesh Baliah 100, 214
Gastroenterologists 153
GCSE subjects 41
General Practitioner in Podiatry
 .... 110, 117
Good references 107
Grace Parfitt 65, 79, 92, 194, 213

H

Hammer toes and bunions 186
Hansen's disease 93
Haydn Kelly 36
Hayley Edginton 147, 150, 151
Health and Care Professional
 Council (HCPC) . 17, 27, 87, 212
Health Education England 101, 165, 207
Heidi Siddle 150
Helen Branthwaite ... 160, 161, 200, 214
High arched foot 161
High-risk 10, 21, 29, 30, 34, 46-7, 55, 60, 63, 74, 79, 80, 89, 94, 125, 133, 147, 150, 152, 153 118, 131, 140, 142, 152, 154
Holistic approach 117, 148, 150
Home visits 125, 129
Hospital directorate 185
Housebound 126, 129
Human movement 52, 55, 62, 74, 181, 205, 207
Hylton B Menz 55

I

Ian Tarr 135, 136, 176, 214
ICATS 132, 207
Imaging 89, 184, 207
Income 170
Independent practice 35, 51, 89, 98, 110, 122, 130, 156, 196, 207, 209
Independent prescribers (I.P) 59, 87, 88, 212
Independent sector ... 16, 28, 29, 51, 79, 84, 85, 108, 116, 122, 123, 125, 130, 131, 147, 156, 162, 167, 169, 171
India 94, 95, 100, 141
Industrial or commercial podiatry
 .... 35, 156, 195
Infection 153
Institute of Chiropodists &
 Podiatrists 3, 80, 82, 185, 202, 207
Irish dance and ballet 180
IRMER 89, 132, 207
Ischaemic 55, 209
Ivan Bristow 86, 214

J

Jai Saxelby 157, 214
James Welch 84
Jennifer Muir 13, 19, 214
Jessica Warner 18, 214
Jill Halstead-Rastrick 100, 176, 200, 214
Jolie Beattie 9, 17
Jonathan Small 35, 158, 214
Journals 106, 107
Judith Watson 24, 118

K

Karl Guttormsen . 32, 143, 166, 214
Kayron Pozo 92
Keith Sands 198
Keratin tissue 54
Keri Hutchinson 88, 197, 213
Kersti Pedar 100
Key dates - podiatry 211
Kidney function 166
Knee injuries 75, 181

L

Langer (UK) 36
Leadership and business 170
Leprosy 55, 93, 94, 95, 208
Limb preservation 154
Limited (Ltd) Company 164
Lisa Farndon 18, 156, 198, 200, 214
Local anaesthetic .23, 26, 56, 62,82, 88, 104, 187
Locum work 35, 162, 163
London Foot Hospital .. 19, 42, 211, 216
Louise Kennedy 9, 126, 127, 214

M

Macmillan Cancer 145
Magnetic resonance scanners 89
Malignancy 113, 120, 124, 208
Management plan. 59, 117
Managers 110, 175, 176
Mandatory training 131
Marathon runners 160, 161, 179
Martin Fox 95, 141, 142, 214
Masters in surgery 184
Masters programme 79
Mature students 27, 48, 79, 110
Measure carbon monoxide 111
Medicine 8, 9, 10, 16, 17, 21, 24, 31, 32, 36, 41, 47, 50, 52, 53, 55, 56, 61, 65, 70, 74, 79, 83, 86, 105, 110, 111, 118, 119, 136, 152, 165, 167, 177, 178, 179, 181, 186, 198, 202, 207, 208, 209, 214, 217
Medicines Act 88
Medico-legal work 189
Membership journal 115
Mentorship 14, 57, 79, 88
Microbiology 120
Microwave treatment 173

Mike Mccolgan 157
Minority representation 100
Modular systems 129
Modules 61
Multi-disciplinary foot care team (MDT) 31, 153, 199
Multiple sclerosis 126
Musculoskeletal (MSK) .28, 55, 64, 119

N

Nail surgery 80, 116
Nancy Keller 68, 213
National Diabetes Foot Care Audit (NDFCA) 137
Nerve pain 186
Neurologists 153
Neuropathy 64, 93, 111, 137, 209
Nursing home 126

O

Objective structured clinical examination (OSCE) 72
Oncologist 117, 144, 208
Orthopaedic surgery 62, 134
Orthopaedics ..31, 50, 89, 131, 134, 135, 157, 181, 185, 186, 187, 208, 209
Orthoses 30, 36, 50, 62, 123, 129, 133, 149, 150, 156, 159, 177, 206, 208
OSGO 36, 202
Overseas students 103
Oxygen flow 72

P

Paediatric patient 83
Pain medication 122
Pathology 50, 53, 55, 66, 69, 89, 113, 119, 120, 152, 183, 208
Paul Haughian .18, 22, 59, 116, 213

Paul Murphy 22, 48, 102, 213
Phd 74, 98, 187, 195, 199, 200, 206, 208, 209
Phil Hendy 58, 81, 196, 197, 214
Phil Vasyli................................. 159
Physics 51
Physiotherapists .. 9, 17, 18, 22, 28, 31, 122, 132-3, 153, 175
Plagiarism 74
Plantar keratoma 199
Plastic skin flap surgery 120
Podiatric surgeons 87, 186
Podiatric surgery 8, 10, 33, 56, 113, 134, 151, 156, 167, 172, 183, 184, 185, 187, 188, 212
Podiatry Rheumatic Care Association. 149
Podo-paediatrics................. 84, 208
Poor healing 126
Prescription only medications.... 88, 134
Presentation skills 197
Pressure measurement......... 56, 139
Primary Care 38, 165
Prison Service 158
Private practice .. 10, 16, 18, 38, 39, 53, 58, 79, 97, 110, 116, 123, 158, 164, 170, 171, 172
Prolotherapy............................. 122
Promoting podiatry 77, 196
Prosected specimens 69
Protocols 133, 137, 172
Psycho-motor skills..................... 52

R

Racial variations 99
Radiological techniques......... 62, 89
Ralph Graham..................... 19, 214
Raymond Robinson...... 38, 58, 101, 194, 214

Research..... 24, 64, 71, 74, 75, 100, 198, 200, 214
Resuscitation................... 62, 72, 81
Rheumatology....... 146, 147-9, 151, 187, 209, 214
Rodrigo Diaz-Martinez............. 129
Role of a University.................... 70
Royal College of Podiatry 3, 37, 80, 82, 83, 84, 104, 149, 184, 185, 188, 192, 202, 208, 209, 212, 217
Running a budget...................... 175
Ryan Brain 46, 47, 74, 213

S

Sarah Reel................................... 64
Sarah Twiss.. 29, 30, 39, 41, 81, 84, 125, 215
Scalpel work 55
Sciences 3, 14, 36, 46, 53, 208, 209
Scotland . 23, 42, 57, 58, 59, 61, 66, 67, 68, 83, 101, 102, 124, 185
Scottish system 20, 68
Sean Savage 180, 215
Shona Wesley 52, 116, 213
Shuja Merban.. 21, 60, 97, 114, 213
Shuropody........... 10, 158, 164, 196
Simon Costain... 179, 180, 181, 215
Simon Otter............ 57, 69, 73, 196
Siobhan Muirhead,.................... 215
Skin .. 17, 21, 23, 29, 30, 46, 49, 50, 54, 56, 60, 62, 82, 85, 94, 111, 117, 118, 119, 120, 122, 124, 139, 150, 152, 156, 171, 173, 205, 206, 207, 208, 209, 210
SMAE Institute 118
Smoking.................................... 111
Social worker 126
Sociology and psychology 53
Socks and shoes 137

Sole Trader-self-employed 164
Statutory sick pay 130
Stephanie Owen 37, 68
Steroid injections 87-8, 122, 147
Stethoscope 143
Steve Kriss 187, 215
Stuart Baird 18, 59, 124, 196
Sub-specialisations 167
Suzy Taylor 154, 176, 215

T

Taster days 196
Tendinopathy 120, 132
The family doctor 25
Tim Kilmartin 19, 117, 183, 187, 200, 215
Tony Blair premiership 101
Tony Gavin 36, 170
Tony Wilkinson 188
Trainee podiatric surgeon 34
Trevor Prior 147, 159, 177, 179, 215

U

Ulcer 29, 94, 128, 144, 147, 152
Ultrasound .. 26, 59, 62, 80, 89, 120, 122, 149, 153, 180, 209
Ultrasound 89, 120, 157, 209
Ultrasound, ... 26, 62, 120
Universities .. 42, 44, 45, 57, 61, 72, 80, 81, 92, 95, 103, 105, 108, 185, 203
Urine 72, 111
USA podiatry 183
Usamah Khalid 10, 33, 100, 183, 184, 185

V

Vascular practitioner 143
Vasculitis 149
Verruca 19, 84, 120
Victoria North 19, 215
Video 77, 123, 173, 192, 193
Vietnam 94
Viva voce 72

W

Walking cycle 49
Wes Vernon 36
Wesley Vernon 192, 193, 215

X

X-rays 24, 121

Z

Zoe Alexander .. 20, 21, 47, 52, 120, 213

Printed in Great Britain
by Amazon